"This mind-body workbook for anger sets the standard for the treatment the entire spectrum of anger management issues, including court mandated treatment for domestic violence offenders. Mind-body bridging is a set of powerful techniques that will help one to rest the system in one's brain (the I-System) that is responsible for unmanaged anger. I have been in practice twenty years and have found that the tools in this workbook are far superior, better accepted, and more quickly effective than any that I have used with court-ordered domestic violence offenders. Long-term follow-up of recidivism showed rates of only eight percent. Further, I have used and continue to use mind-body bridging in my own life with transformational results."

—**Kevin Webb, MSW, LCSW**, clinical consultant and the
Utah Division of Child and Family Services

"Stan and Carolyn have done it again. *The Mind-Body Workbook for Anger* is a user-friendly, easy-to-apply solution to the problem of anger management. In my long career in treating domestic violence offenders, no other method or technique can compare with it. This book should be on top of the list for both therapists and clients."

—**Jules Shuzen Harris, EdD**, author of *Anger: It Has Something to Teach Us: Can We Listen*

"As a psychotherapist, I have been actively involved with domestic violence coalitions and treatment agencies. Anger-management treatment programs based on this *Mind-Body Workbook for Anger* dramatically reduce dropout rates and recidivism in comparison with conventional treatment methods. In fact, with the favorable results of a large randomized control trial awaiting publication, mind-body bridging is en route to becoming the first evidenced-based treatment and best practice for domestic violence offenders."

—**Isaac Phillips, MSW, LCSW**, executive director of Equinox Counseling
Services; co-chair of the Salt Lake Area Domestic Violence Coalition;
and member of the Utah Council for Domestic Violence Perpetrator Treatment

"Research I conducted with domestic violence offenders using mind-body bridging as an intervention found the offenders experienced less stress; gained greater access to problem-solving abilities; and improved their relationships with partners, children, and co-workers. The mind-body bridging approach helped these at-risk individuals avoid reoffending largely by sharpening ability to recognize internal triggers. In my experience, the mind-body bridging techniques used in the *Mind-Body Workbook for Anger* are successful because they are practical, straightforward, and allow individuals to see results immediately."

—**Elisa Audo, PhD**, author *The Experience of Mind-Body Bridging as a Treatment for Offenders of Domestic Violence*, doctoral dissertation, California Institute of Integral Studies, 2012, San Francisco, CA

MIND-BODY WORKBOOK for anger

Effective Tools for Anger Management & Conflict Resolution

STANLEY H. BLOCK, MD
& CAROLYN BRYANT BLOCK
with ANDREA A. PETERS

NEW HARBINGER PUBLICATIONS, INC.

Distributed in Canada by Raincoast Books

Copyright © 2013 by Stanley H. Block and Carolyn Bryant Block
New Harbinger Publications, Inc.
5674 Shattuck Avenue
Oakland, CA 94609
www.newharbinger.com

Cover design by Amy Shoup
Acquired by Jess O'Brien
Edited by Nelda Street

Library of Congress Cataloging-in-Publication Data on file

Printed in the United States of America

15   14   13
10   9   8   7   6   5   4   3   2   1   First printing

CONTENTS

FOREWORD

Emotion dysregulation has led to an incomprehensible tally of negative consequences for individuals, couples, families, and communities. It follows, then, that an intervention capable of effectively and efficiently helping people regulate their emotions holds enormous potential to alleviate suffering. It is this potential that led me to encourage my colleague Dr. Stanley Block to publish a workbook that applies his mind-body treatment approach, "mind-body bridging," to that form of emotion dysregulation that we refer to as "anger." I have eagerly anticipated the publication of this workbook, because I have personally witnessed how mind-body bridging empowers individuals to change their lives and relationships for the better. I have published empirical research that supports the effectiveness of mind-body bridging for domestic violence offenders (Tollefson et al. 2009). I have applied mind-body bridging in my clinical practice with domestic violence offenders and other clients who experience problems with emotion regulation. I have also integrated mind-body bridging into my own life. Through these experiences, I have come to greatly appreciate how mind-body bridging can change lives in ways that lead to lasting personal and relational fulfillment.

This workbook will help individuals learn how to apply mind-body bridging to resolve emotion regulation problems, including anger. I use the word "resolve" purposely: mind-body bridging is not an anger management *strategy*; if applied correctly, it is an *intervention* that will eliminate destructive and dysfunctional forms of emotion dysregulation, including anger. Consequently, this workbook can be used in anger management groups or by anyone who could benefit from improved emotion regulation. This workbook is particularly well suited to intervention programs for domestic violence offenders, given that research has shown that most abusers suffer from some form of extreme body tension and emotion dysregulation (Dutton and Sonkin 2002; Rosenberg 2003). Thus, improving emotion regulation is critical to successful domestic violence treatment.

Mind-body bridging holds that the key factor in understanding the root cause of dysfunctional or destructive behavior like domestic violence lies in understanding the mind-body state of the person prior to the aggressive outburst (for example, thoughts spinning wildly, body numb and full of tension, narrowed awareness of surroundings). This mind-body state is likely to explode into a violent outburst. When individuals are asked what sets off this explosive state, the array of answers may include: "She doesn't appreciate how hard I work," "She knows I can't stand a dirty kitchen," "It's his sarcastic tone of voice," or "The kid left the bike in the driveway." Mind-body bridging asserts that the explosive state is the result of the overactivity of a system in our body called the "Identity System," which functions by constructing and maintaining a thought picture of how we and the world should be at any given moment. These thoughts are called "requirements" (for example, *I should feel rested when I wake in the morning, My wife should always be in a good mood, My partner should make me breakfast on my birthday,* and so on). When requirements are frustrated, the Identity System works in a way that creates mental commotion, clutters the mind, tenses the body, and constricts awareness. This interferes with not only the functions of the mind but also physical functions, such as pulse, blood pressure, digestion, cellular metabolism, hormone regulation, and nervous system functioning. Mind-body bridging is a simple technique for resting the Identity System, which in turn *resolves* the explosive state (for example, dysfunctional or abusive behavior). In other words, when we free ourselves from the effects of the Identify System, we literally switch from using the "fight or flight" network in the brain to the "executive functioning" network. This network, sometimes referred to as the "natural functioning" network of the brain, is capable of effective, functional problem solving, whereas the "fight or flight" network is not. Rather, decisions and actions made using this part of the brain often lead to dysfunctional, even disastrous consequences.

Users of this workbook will learn and apply key mind-body bridging principles and skills. They will also evaluate and track their progress at the end of each chapter. In the first chapter readers will learn how to quiet the Identity System, put the executive functioning network of the brain firmly in control, and regulate their emotional states. In the second chapter, readers will learn how to recognize and disarm their requirements, particularly those that trigger the Identity System and result in emotion dysregulation. The third chapter teaches readers how to recognize and manage a component of the Identify System called the "depressor," which is responsible for negative self-talk or "storylines" that fuel the Identity System. In chapter 4 readers learn about the "fixer" component of the Identity System and how to stop it from infecting them with perfectionistic thinking (for example, *It's all or nothing, It has to be this way or else*). Chapter 5 focuses on helping the reader live a life free from the destructive influence of requirements. Readers will learn how to free themselves from requirements, using a powerful tool called "mind mapping." In the remaining four chapters, readers will learn how to use the knowledge and skills they have developed to improve relationships with loved ones, friends, coworkers, and others; improve physical and mental health; and regulate emotional states in virtually any situation, including moments of crisis.

In summary, this workbook will transform lives, as readers learn and apply mind-body bridging principles and skills. These principles and skills can free us from the disabling effects of the Identity System and allow the natural, or executive, functioning network of the brain to help us effectively cope with life stressors, overcome challenges, and achieve a state of harmony and balance in life.

—Derrik R. Tollefson, PhD
Associate Professor of Social Work, College of Social Work at the
University of Utah and Utah State University

ACKNOWLEDGMENTS

Our teaching about anger management is primarily influenced by the effective way that individuals suffering from unmanaged anger have shared with us how they used mind-body bridging to liberate themselves from the restrictions of the I-System. Although we have not specifically referenced other workers in the anger management field, we appreciate their pioneering work. The clinicians from around the world using, developing, and refining mind-body bridging have our gratitude. Deserving of specific mention are the members of the International Mind-Body Bridging Certification Committee: Don Glover, Rich Landward, Theresa McCormick, Andrea Phillips, Isaac Phillips, and Kevin Webb. The research efforts of Yoshi Nakamura, David Lipschitz, and Derrik Tollefson to establish a firm evidence basis for mind-body bridging is much appreciated. Carol Ann Kent, the MBB coordinator, has ably assisted in the preparation of this workbook. The direction from the editors of New Harbinger Publications was most helpful.

INTRODUCTION

When you can't manage your anger, your anger becomes a destructive force that affects the quality of your life. It harms your relationships, destroys your accomplishments, and even affects your health. In this book, you will see the underlying cause of your angry outbursts: the *Identity System*. You will learn tools that you can use step by step to not only remove that root cause, but also transform that angry state back to one of vitality and vigor, which is the backbone of a creative, constructive, and fulfilling life. These tools have been found to work well when used for dealing with anger day to day, and even for the complex cases of people who have had problems with domestic violence (Tollefson et al. 2009).

ANGER

Anger, a natural human emotion, becomes a problem only when you are unable to manage it without hurting yourself or others, or damaging things. It's a strong feeling evoked by perceived injury that often comes with a desire to take revenge or get back at someone. The tendency of anger to veer out of control is clearly shown by its Latin root word: *angere*, to strangle. Anger that you don't handle in a healthy way strangles, suppresses, restricts, and harms those around you, and prevents you from living your best life. The angry outburst may range from speaking cross words, raising your voice, and losing your temper to verbal abuse, bullying, and violent actions. The English language has a series of words used to describe these angry mind-body states, ranging from *adaptive* to *maladaptive*: annoyed, displeased, irritated, peeved, cross, bitter, resentful, stirred up, worked up, teed off, heated up, fuming, ranting, raving, agitated, roaring, and violent.

Since anger is a natural, adaptive human emotion, why is anger so hard to manage? Maybe you have been doing your best, but nothing you've tried has lasted very long. You may even have the false belief that something is wrong with you because of your inability to control your anger. What you haven't yet discovered is that you are fully equipped to moderate and control your anger.

IDENTITY SYSTEM (I-SYSTEM)

The holistic system that regulates mind-body states is called the "I-System." It's either active (on) or at rest (off) (Block and Block 2007; Block and Block 2010; Block and Block 2012). The I-System is active when you are upset, resent others, or feel angry. You know it's on when your mind is cluttered with spinning angry or "get even" thoughts, your body is tense, and all that you are aware of is the target in front of you. This holistic system is called the "I-System," because when it's on, all of us falsely *identify with* the contents of our spinning thoughts and the physical distress the I-System causes. It is crucial to notice the I-System, because when it's active, your body's natural way of working is disrupted. When you have feelings of being driven toward abusing someone verbally or physically, realize that it's *always* your I-System (not what's going on around you and not the other person) that is clouding your judgment and prompting you to explode. Once the I-System is active, you live your daily life as if you were seeing the world through the distorted prism of your I-System.

MIND-BODY BRIDGING

Mind-body bridging is an easy way to put the I-System to rest or, in other words, to cool down your heated-up mind-body state. When your I-System is calm, you are able to successfully deal with your anger (Tollefson et al. 2009).

Mind-body bridging may, at first, seem like existing cognitive restructuring approaches, mindfulness training, trigger identification, and grounding skills used in dialectical behavior therapy (DBT) (Linehan 1993), cognitive behavioral therapy (CBT) (Beck 1995), mindfulness-based stress reduction (MBSR) (Williams et al. 2007), and other therapy approaches. But there are many ways in which they differ. The major premise in mind-body bridging is that we are always connected to a wellspring of healing, goodness, and wisdom (whole, complete, and without damage). The reason for our harmful actions is that when the I-System is active, it keeps us from reaching into and expressing this personal wellspring. Using mind-body bridging tools quiets the I-System, by reducing a stress biomarker (Lipschitz et al., 2013), so that our skills for managing our anger quickly grow, which allows us to make the right choices in the moment.

BRAIN BASIS

Brain research (Weissman et al. 2006) has found two networks of functioning with different features: an executive network and a default-mode network. The *executive network* coordinates moment by moment how we see the world, think, make decisions, and act. It's responsible for the direction and management of our lives. The *default-mode network* is at work when we're having exaggerated thoughts about ourselves and our experiences, making it difficult to respond appropriately to situations as they come up. Researchers have found that when the default-mode network is active, the executive network is inactive (Boly, Phillips, Balteau, et al. 2008). Only one network can be in the driver's seat at a time.

Using *fMRI*, scientists and doctors can now take pictures of how the brain changes while it's busy. Shaun Ho (Block, Ho, and Nakamura 2009) suggests that the I-System refers to the default-mode network and that mind-body bridging refers to the executive network. Brain research (Boly, Phillips, Tshibanda, et al. 2008) shows that when the default-mode network is not active, your executive network takes charge, regulating your mind so that you function at your best. The I-System is why you can't seem to manage your anger; it makes you explode in angry outbursts (Lee, Uken, and Sebold 2004). Mind-body bridging quiets the I-System, letting you manage your anger and naturally function in executive mode.

Imagine a big switch in your brain that turns the I-System (default-mode network) on and off. When the I-System is on, it shuts down your executive functioning. When the switch is off, you function naturally, manage your anger, and live life at its best.

MIND-BODY LANGUAGE

Your mind and body do not function without each other; they work as a single unit that you can't separate (the *mind-body*). You will learn a clinically validated mind-body language that allows you to know, connect with, and manage your mind and body as never before. This easy-to-understand language frames your mind-body states in terms of an active or inactive I-System. This gives you the power to quickly start reducing your angry outbursts and harmful actions.

There are times when life is overwhelming. Your head is full of urgent and pressing angry thoughts, your body is full of tension, and you can't see the light at the end of the tunnel. This state of mind and body is the *powerless self*. The powerless self is not simply a mental state; it also affects every cell of your body. It's caused by the activity of your I-System, not the stressors in your life. This powerless self leads to a reactive state with possible explosive outbursts and actions that are abusive and inappropriate.

This workbook is based on the fact that your *mind-body* (mind and body as a whole unit) knows how to simply and quickly deal with the stressors in your life without resorting to angry outbursts. This mind-body state is your *natural self* functioning in executive mode. When you use the anger-reduction tools in this book, you will soon find that you come to a state of natural harmony and balance in your life, where appropriate action takes place. Each chapter lists the new mind-body language used in that chapter.

HOW TO USE THIS BOOK

This workbook is simple and easy to use. Mind-body bridging principles are stated at the beginning of each chapter. You then validate them for yourself through quick, guided, experiential exercises that give you a unique insight into your mind and body as a whole. At the end of each chapter, the anger-reduction tools taught in that chapter are listed so that you can use them in your daily life. Each chapter serves as a building block for the next one, so it's important to do the exercises and read each chapter in sequence. As you move through the chapters, your list of anger-reduction tools keeps growing so that you can rely on them for anything that's going on in your life.

You will find an MBB (mind-body bridging) Quality of Life Gauge at the beginning, middle, and end of the book, which will help you to measure how your life changes. At the end of each chapter is an MBB Rating Scale that lets you know how well you're using in your daily life the anger-reduction tools you are learning. When you use your tools in your life every day, you'll be able to manage your anger and reduce conflicts, because your natural self will be in the driver's seat.

CHAPTER 1

USE YOUR EXECUTIVE FUNCTIONING TO CONTROL ANGER

Principles

The active I-System makes it hard for you to control your anger.

When your I-System is resting, you will handle daily life without angry outbursts.

Mind-Body Language

I-System: Each of us has an I-System, and it's either active (on) or resting (off). You know the I-System is active when your mind is cluttered with spinning thoughts, your body is tense, and you are getting irritated and angry. It's called the "I-System" because it prompts you to falsely identify with the spinning thoughts and the physical distress the it causes.

Natural self: How you think, feel, see the world, and act when your I-System is resting and you are functioning in executive mode. Your mind and body work in harmony as a unit, and stressors are handled smoothly and quickly, without angry outbursts.

Mind-body bridging: When you use the tools in this workbook, you form a bridge from your active I-System (where angry outbursts happen) to your natural self in executive mode (where daily life is handled in a smooth and healthy way).

YOUR ANGRY REACTION TO A PROBLEM

1. Let's get started so you can experience the first two principles for yourself. Think of a problem that makes you angry and ready to explode. Write it in the oval below. It may be helpful to look at the sample map on the next page. Now, take a couple of minutes to write down around the oval any thoughts that come to mind about the problem. Be as specific as possible. Work quickly, without self-editing.

ANGRY REACTION MAP

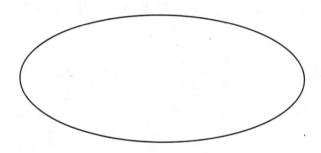

A. Is your mind clear or cluttered with thoughts?

_____

B. Is your body tense or relaxed? List where and how your body is tense:

_____

_____

C. With your mind and body in this condition, how do you act?

_____

You probably think that it's the problem that's creating your inner distress and anger that you see on your map. It's not! You have just experienced your active I-System. Your I-System takes a difficult problem, creates mind clutter and body tension, and restricts your ability to act without angry outbursts. The next map allows you to see what is causing your anger, and it will teach you the critical first step in managing your anger.

SAMPLE MAP: ANGRY REACTION

She calls my friends losers.

She should keep the kids quiet.

SHE DOESN'T RESPECT ME

She shouldn't be so critical.

She shouldn't complain when I drink beer and watch football.

She and the kids would be on the streets if it weren't for me.

She should do what I tell her to do.

A. Is your mind clear or cluttered with thoughts?

My mind is cluttered with thoughts about getting no respect.

B. Is your body tense or relaxed? List where and how your body is tense.

Band around my head, fists clenched, really tense all over.

C. With your mind and body in this condition, how do you act?

Irritable, angry, yelling

2. The next part of this exercise can change your life forever, because it shows you how to get your I-System to rest. For this important map, it's helpful to be in a room without distractions such as people talking, TV, or electronic devices. Write that same problem (the one you wrote in the oval on the first map) in the oval below. Before you continue, seat yourself comfortably, listen to any background sounds, feel the pressure of your body on your seat, feel your feet on the floor, and feel the pen in your hand. Take your time. If you have thoughts, gently return to listening to the background sounds and tuning in to your senses. Once you feel settled, start writing whatever comes to mind about the problem. Watch the ink go onto the paper, keep feeling the pen in your hand, and listen to any background sounds. Write for a couple of minutes.

ANGRY REACTION MAP WITH BRIDGING

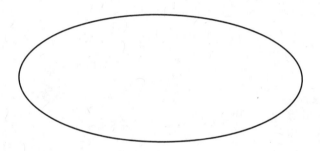

A. Is your mind clear or cluttered with thoughts?

_____

B. Is your body tense or relaxed?

_____

C. How is this map different from the first one you made?

_____

D. How would you act in this mind-body state?

_____

E. If you could live your life with your mind-body in this state, do you think your life would be better?
Yes _____No_____

The exercise you just did is called *mind-body mapping*. These two-part mind-body maps are short written exercises that take just a few minutes. Mapping is a snapshot of your ability to control your anger, and it opens the door to your natural self as it functions in executive mode.

Take a look at what differs between your two completed maps. Your first map shows your I-System in action. In the second map, you got to see what it's like to have a quiet I-System. You experienced that when you literally come to your senses by focusing on your body sensations and the sounds around you, the I-System automatically quiets, your body tension eases, and your ability to control your anger increases. You have just experienced the dramatic shift out of a mind-body state in which your I-System was clouding your judgment, overwhelming your body with tension, and closing down your ability to control your feelings and actions. Mind-body bridging uses the mind and the body to move you from a place where you could explode into an angry outburst, to your natural self as it functions in executive mode. Remember, your natural self is how you think, feel, see the world, and act when your I-System is resting.

When you did the first map, your angry thoughts were spinning and your body was tense, which makes it hard for you to handle tough situations without being angry. When you quiet your I-System, as you did in the second map, you become more settled and can better handle problems in a healthy way (as shown in figure 1.1 on the next page). Note that the size of the problem hasn't changed. When you have trouble managing your anger, you come to believe that you are a small vessel and that you can only use a small portion of your executive functioning ability. Simply by quieting your I-System, you become a bigger vessel. Your space to manage your anger and solve problems expands with mind-body bridging so that your natural state resumes. This analogy of having a larger space to deal with life's challenges is *exactly* how mind-body bridging works. You can now deal with your responsibilities quickly and in a healthy way, without angry and harmful outcomes. Your ability to handle daily life by using executive functioning builds naturally. Keep in mind that you don't have to force yourself to function naturally; this will develop on its own. It is your birthright.

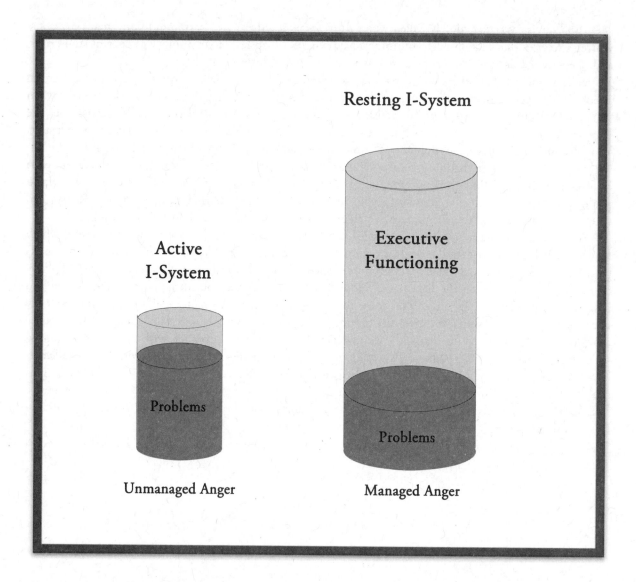

Figure 1.1 Which vessel are you in?

When you feel angry and irritable, your ability to handle problems (the darkly shaded space) is greatly reduced, as if you were a small vessel. This allows you to only use a fraction of your executive functioning (lightly shaded area). When your I-System is active, you feel stuck, and this stops you from being able to manage your anger.

You automatically become a bigger vessel when the I-System is resting. The problems haven't changed, but the space inside the vessel has changed. The lightly shaded area in the larger vessel (which refers to your natural state and your ability to manage anger) expands as you switch off your I-System.

MBB QUALITY OF LIFE GAUGE

Date: _____

It's time to fill out your first MBB Quality of Life Gauge. This scale is repeated throughout the workbook so that you can measure your progress and keep track of your life-changing experiences. Think back over the past week as you fill out the chart.

Circle the number under your answer.	Not at all	Several days	More than half the days	Nearly every day
1. I've had positive interest and pleasure in my activities.	0	1	3	5
2. I've felt optimistic, excited, and hopeful.	0	1	3	5
3. I've slept well and woken up feeling refreshed.	0	1	3	5
4. I've had lots of energy.	0	1	3	5
5. I've been able to focus on tasks and use self-discipline.	0	1	3	5
6. I've stayed healthy, eaten well, exercised, and had fun.	0	1	3	5
7. I've felt good about my relationships with my family and friends.	0	1	3	5
8. I've been satisfied with my accomplishments at home, work, or school.	0	1	3	5
9. I've been comfortable with my financial situation.	0	1	3	5
10. I've felt good about the spiritual base of my life.	0	1	3	5
11. I've been satisfied with the direction of my life.	0	1	3	5
12. I've felt fulfilled, with a sense of well-being and peace of mind.	0	1	3	5
Column Total	___	___	___	___

Score Key:

0-15 . . . . Poor

16-30 . . . . .Fair   Total Score _____

31-45 . . . . .Good

46 and above. Excellent

ANGER REDUCTION TOOLS

Remember the mapping exercise? When you did the first map, you explored a problem that made you angry. The second map allowed you to explore that same problem with a calmer body and clearer mind. Maybe this state lasted for a while, or maybe it was brief. When you made your second map, what pulled you away from hearing the background sounds, feeling the pen, and seeing the ink go onto the paper? Yes, it was your thoughts. The I-System spins your thoughts, makes your body tense, and closes you off from your senses. It converts stressful situations into inner distress and anger. Thought labeling and bridging awareness practices are the tools you will learn in this chapter to help you prevent explosive outbursts.

Thought Labeling

Your mind naturally makes both positive and negative thoughts. You will never get rid of your negative thoughts. In fact, trying to get rid of them doesn't work, because when you push them away, you give them even more energy.

When angry thoughts come up, it helps to label them using an anger reduction tool called *thought labeling*. Thought labeling lets you see that a thought is *just a thought*. This prevents the I-System from taking a thought, spinning a story from it, crossing the mind-body connection, and creating body tension. Once this happens, the thought is no longer just a thought, but a state of mind-body distress that can lead to an angry and explosive outburst.

Let's see how thought labeling works. Think of something that upsets you; for example, *My boss always criticizes me.* When that tension-filled thought pops into your mind, say to yourself, *I'm having the thought, "My boss always criticizes me."* Some people even continue with *and a thought is just a thought.* This helps reinforce that what is now making you upset is not your boss, but your thoughts about your boss. This recognition that a thought is just a thought is one of the tools that will help you stop your I-System from capturing your thoughts.

Skip, a football coach, was referred to mind-body bridging because of road rage. When other drivers failed to honor "Skip's rules of the road," he would become furious, follow them, and, a number of times, pull up beside them and yell while pumping his fist. If he got the other driver to stop, Skip would get out of his car, start cussing at the person, and begin pounding and kicking the other driver's car.

Skip was very macho and belittled using his senses, calling it "too feminine." But he liked the idea of being able to control his thoughts, so he began to build the habit of labeling his thoughts. One day while driving, he reported, "A lightbulb went on in my head. I could kill someone if I carried out those thoughts." Thought labeling gave him the tool to be "boss" of his thoughts. Now, when he is driving and someone cuts in front of him, and he has thoughts like *How can he do that? That SOB—he needs to suffer* (which used to lead to his angry and destructive behavior), Skip says to himself, *I'm having the thought, "How could he do that."* Skip continues to label his thoughts, which calms him down so that he's no longer a danger to himself or others. He has also begun doing the bridging awareness practices, and not only has his road rage stopped, but his life has become more productive and satisfying.

Use thought labeling to manage your anger. During the day, when an angry thought pulls you away from what you are doing, label that thought and become aware of your activity again. For example, when you're in the shower and the thought *I hate my job* pops into your mind, say to yourself, *I am having the thought "I hate my job,"* return to taking your shower, sense the water on your body, and hear the sounds of the shower.

Bridging Awareness Practices

When the I-System is active, it closes off your senses until all you are aware of is your anger. It's like putting your hands over your ears to block out any other sound. The I-System not only keeps you from hearing the ever-present background sounds, but also keeps you from experiencing your ever-present natural self. When you use your senses, your I-System quiets, letting you deal with your challenges with a calm, ready mind and a relaxed body.

Bridging awareness practices use your senses to build a bridge from a life filled with anger (the powerless self of the I-System) to life lived at its best (the natural self of executive functioning). Building this bridge is easier than you think.

Jimmy, a nine-year-old with a diagnosis of autism spectrum disorder, wasn't able to ride public transportation because of his uncontrollable angry outbursts when he did not get "his seat." After a number of attempts, his mother gave up trying to take Jimmy on the bus. This greatly limited their lives. Then his mother learned the mind-body bridging tools in this workbook. Finding the bridging awareness practices to be effective for relieving her stress, she patiently taught Jimmy to slowly rub the fabric of his shirtsleeve and to *feel* what that was like. With the guidance of his mother, Jimmy began to sense what he touched throughout the day. His temper tantrums at home diminished. Soon thereafter, they tried to ride the bus once again. This time, upon taking a seat, Jimmy immediately began to rub the fabric of his shirt slowly. Now, they are able to ride the bus, even when Jimmy doesn't get "his seat"!

AWARENESS OF BACKGROUND SOUNDS

Your environment is full of sounds. During the day, pause and listen to any background sounds, like the white noise of the heating or air-conditioning system, the wind blowing, traffic sounds, or the hum of the refrigerator. If your thoughts start to spin, label them and gently return your awareness to what you were doing. See what happens to your mind and body when you focus on background sounds.

Bill was in a mind-body bridging program for domestic violence offenders. He immediately found the bridging awareness practices helpful. In fact, he shared multiple examples of how they had helped him "quiet down" his angry mind and body. He shared the following incident. It was on the weekend, and for a whole series of reasons, he felt wound up. Ready to explode, he was about to begin an argument with his wife. Suddenly he heard a dog barking, and as he put it, "I came to my senses, felt a calmness coming over me, and saw the clock face showing 12:05 p.m. Then out of my mouth came, 'Dear, it's noon. Let me make us some sandwiches.'" Over lunch they discussed and resolved the issue that was bothering Bill. What was striking to Bill was that he had never before made lunch, and he couldn't get over how, as he put it, "the kindness popped out of me."

AWARENESS OF WHAT YOU ARE TOUCHING

We all touch hundreds of things every day. Were you aware of how it felt under your fingertips today when you touched your shoes, socks, shirt, keys, fork, watch, paper, cell phone, or computer? Were you aware of your senses when you touched your child or a close friend? Did you sense the warmth of the coffee cup or the coldness of the water bottle in your hand? Chances are you didn't. Your I-System has numbed your body, detaching you from your senses. Tuning in to your sense of touch is another bridging awareness practice that quiets your I-System.

Be aware of what the sensations are like under your fingertips as you touch things like glasses, phones, pens, keys, computers, and other objects. Are these surfaces smooth or rough, cold or warm, pleasant or unpleasant? When washing your hands or showering, feel the water as it touches your skin. Sense what it's like to touch others or be touched. This may take some effort, because the I-System dulls your senses. A young, highly stressed student told us that simply sensing his thumb rubbing against his finger calmed him down enough to stop him from getting angry with his teachers and classmates.

Note what you touch and the sensations you feel during the day. Do you feel more settled when you are aware of what you are touching? Keep practicing!

AWARENESS OF COLORS, FACIAL FEATURES, AND SHAPES

The I-System grasps at certain images while rejecting others. This prevents you from seeing the whole picture. When you use one or more of your senses, the I-System calms down, your awareness expands, and you actually *see* what's out there. When you look at a sunset or even a speck of dust on the floor, does your busy head let you see its colors, shapes, and uniqueness? Probably not for long. Take a look at your next meal. When your food is in front of you, really look at it before you eat. What textures are there? What are the shapes? What color is your food?

Lois, a successful fashion designer, was "totally stressed out" when her well-behaved eleven-year-old twin boys ganged up with her teenage daughter. They all refused to do their homework, broke curfew, and created havoc at home. Lois was upset and angry: "All I saw was red." After learning mind-body bridging, she calmed her I-System by focusing on the background colors of the walls, ceiling, sky, and so forth. This quieted her I-System; she said, "I became collected and started making better decisions. Rather than 'seeing red,' I saw clearly what to do."

Pay attention today to what you see when you look at scenery and objects. Notice their colors, shapes and forms. Pay attention to the facial expressions of the people around you: family, friends, coworkers, and even strangers. When you have an angry thought, label it *just a thought* and gently return to whatever you were doing. When you really *see* what's out there, your I-System quiets, and your appreciation of life expands as your anger fades.

AWARENESS OF YOUR BODY

The *proprioception system* is a vital part of your nervous system that informs you about your posture, the way you move, and the degree to which your muscles contract. The tense muscles you noticed in the first exercise were due to the I-System getting in the way of the natural functioning of the proprioception system. Your natural functioning is signaling for the muscle to relax, but your I-System takes over that normal response and tightens up the muscle even further. This is an example of how the I-System works to disrupt mind-body harmony. Another example is responding to an injury that causes pain. The acute pain is a signal to take action right away. After a few minutes, the central nervous system sets up a barrier to reduce the pain signals so that you are better able to carry on with your daily life. In many people with chronic pain, the I-System removes the barrier so that the intense pain remains for weeks, months, or even years, getting in the way of their daily lives and things they need to do.

Amy lost her well-paying job at a large company due to downsizing. Not being able to find a comparable position, she finally found a lower paying job to cover her rent. Consequently, she was unable to make the payments on her new car, so it was repossessed. As she walked to work every day, Amy became frustrated and angry. When her angry attitude started to affect her job, a coworker suggested mind-body bridging. Amy began using the bridging awareness tools, which you have learned about in this chapter, to calm her I-System. She used the motion of her body (the swing of her arms, her feet hitting the pavement, and the feeling of gravity) and thought labeling as she walked to work. Now, instead of arriving at work tense and angry, she arrives relaxed and ready to face her day.

Let's see how this works. Start leaning slowly to the left. Do you feel the muscle tension in your side? Do you sense the imbalance in your head? Do you sense how your natural functioning wants to correct the imbalance? Lift up your right arm and hold it in midair. Do you feel the pull of gravity? Yes, that's your proprioception system at work. It gives you information about the position of your body in space and the state of your muscles. You use that natural flow of information to automatically move and navigate. Pay attention to gravity as you lift an object or as you get up from a chair. Gravity is your friend; it's always there. Sensing gravity quiets the I-System and grounds you in the present moment.

PUTTING IT ALL TOGETHER

Use your anger reduction tools to manage your anger and to stay relaxed and focused throughout the day. When your thoughts begin to wander from what you are doing, label your thoughts to bring you back to the task at hand. When you have irritability, anger, or body tension (as you had on the first map), know that an angry outburst could result, and use your bridging awareness tools. Notice how your body automatically relaxes and your breathing becomes natural without your having to force it. You are now in direct communication with your mind-body. For example, while you are cooking, listen to the stove's exhaust fan, and you will find that your other senses automatically open. You smell the soup, you see the colors of the vegetables, and your sense of calm expands. By expanding your awareness, you are better able to be sensitive and show compassion for others as you reduce your angry outbursts.

We all know that driving can be a stressful experience that can lead to angry outbursts, especially in heavy traffic and construction delays, and around unsafe drivers. When you are driving, keep the radio, music player, and cell phone off. Note what happens to your body tension as you feel the steering wheel, hear the roar and feel the vibrations of the engine, feel the seat belt across your chest, see the scenery, and pay attention to the road. When angry thoughts pull you away from your driving, label them. Many people have reported to us that these anger reduction tools have literally saved their lives. Others report that their uncontrollable road rage has abated.

As you are falling asleep tonight, listen to and focus on background sounds. Feel and rub the sheets with your fingers. See the darkness when your eyes are closed. Be patient and keep returning to your senses. The busy head can never settle the busy head. If angry and stressful thoughts keep you awake, label your thoughts; for example, say to yourself, *I'm having the thought, "I'll never get to sleep"* or *I'm having the thought, "She'll never change, so what else is new?"* and then return to your senses for a good night's sleep. These anger reduction tools (using your senses and thought labeling) stop the activities of the I-System from robbing you of restful sleep. The quality of your sleep is an important component in managing anger. Improving sleep using mind-body bridging is very effective (Nakamura et al. 2011; Nakamura et al. 2013).

Anger Reduction Tools

➤ Recognize when your I-System is active or inactive.

➤ Use thought labeling.

➤ Use bridging awareness practices:

- Awareness of background sounds

- Awareness of what you are touching

- Awareness of colors, facial features, shapes

- Awareness of your body sensations

You may ask yourself, *Can labeling my thoughts, listening to background sounds, seeing facial features, feeling my feet on the ground, and being aware of what I touch really help me to control my anger and live a better life? Can it really be so simple?* When you make a habit of using these tools to reduce anger, all the cells in your body will give you a resounding yes! So, feel your foot as it touches the ground, sense your fingers on the computer keys, hear the background sounds, feel the pressure on your behind as you sit, feel the fork in your hand, look at your food, and be aware of how the broom moves the dust when you sweep. When your angry thoughts pull you away from what you are doing, label them and return to your task.

After using these tools for a couple of days, return to this page, and fill out the following chart and then the MBB Rating Scale that is on the next page.

Difficult Situation	I-System: Active or Inactive	Thought Labeling	Bridging Awareness Tools	What Happened
Thinking about my critical boss when I was showering	*Active*	*I'm having the thought that my boss is critical*	*Paid attention to the sounds of the shower*	*Tension dropped, able to calmly get ready for work*

Have you noticed that besides reducing anger and irritability, using these tools as part of your daily routine helps you to enjoy life more and be more productive? These tools for reducing anger serve as the basis for the entire workbook. The stronger your mind-body bridging practices, the easier it will be to manage your anger. The following MBB Rating Scale is a way to gauge your progress that lets you know how solid your foundation is.

MBB RATING SCALE
USE YOUR EXECUTIVE FUNCTIONING TO CONTROL ANGER

Date: _____

After using the tools in this chapter for a few days, check the box below that best describes your practice for each question: hardly ever, sometimes, usually, or almost always.

How often do you...	Hardly Ever	Sometimes	Usually	Almost Always
Listen to background sounds?				
Sense the sensations in your fingers when holding your water bottle, coffee cup, a cold glass of water, or a soda can?				
Sense the sensations in your fingers when you touch things throughout the day?				
Experience pressure on your feet when you walk?				
Experience pressure on your behind as you sit?				
Feel the steering wheel, hear the roar of the engine, and pay attention to the road when you are driving?				
Hear the water going down the drain and feel it on your body when you shower or wash your hands?				
Become keenly aware of daily activities like making the bed, eating, brushing your teeth, and lifting?				
Become aware of your body sensations when you touch others?				
Become keenly aware of others' facial expressions?				
Use anger reduction tools to help you defuse situations at home and at work?				
Use bridging awareness and thought labeling tools to help you sleep?				
Use anger reduction tools to reduce stress?				
Sense that you are connected to your own wellspring of healing, goodness, and wisdom?				
Know when your I-System is active (on) or inactive (off)?				

List two new things you've noticed about your life after starting to use your anger reduction tools:

_____

_____

CHAPTER 2

IMPROVE EVERYDAY LIFE BY RECOGNIZING REQUIREMENTS

Principles

Requirements turn on the I-System, restrict your natural self, and set the stage for angry outbursts.

When you recognize requirements, you calm the I-System, reduce your anger, and improve your everyday life.

Mind-Body Language

Requirements: Thoughts made into mental rules by your I-System that tell you how you and the world should be in each moment. When your I-System rules are broken, you become upset and angry.

Recognize requirements: When you become clearly aware that *your requirement*, not the events around you, is making your I-System active, you reduce your anger and function in executive mode.

HOW THE I-SYSTEM WORKS

A lot of systems regulate our bodies. For instance, we have a system that regulates our temperature, keeping the body at around 98.6 degrees Fahrenheit. If our temperature goes up, we sweat, and if it goes down, we shiver as our system tries to get back to the body's normal temperature. In the same way, we all have an I-System. It works like the system that regulates our temperature, but instead of an ideal temperature, the I-System creates an "ideal picture" (requirement) of how you and the world should be. Each moment, both systems sense whether their requirements are met. When the requirement of the system that regulates temperature is not fulfilled, we shiver or sweat. When something comes up that doesn't fulfill the I-System requirement, our I-System becomes active, and we have body tension, mind clutter, stress, and a tough time controlling our anger.

The natural state of the I-System is to rest. It's only turned on when requirements are unfulfilled. Remember, requirements are rules that your I-System has created for you about how you and the world should be at any moment (for example, *I should be able to control my anger, My boss shouldn't raise his voice,* or *My partner should be more understanding*).

It's vital to know the difference between thoughts that are natural expectations and those that are made into requirements. All thoughts are natural and start free of the I-System's influence. It's not what the thought is about (the content), but what happens to the thought, that makes it a requirement. For example, *I should have a good job* and *My partner should be faithful* are thoughts or expectations you would naturally have. When the I-System makes them into requirements (rules) and something happens that breaks those rules, this creates body tension and mental stress, and makes it hard for you to handle the situation. You are now more apt to lose control of your anger. When a thought is not a requirement, you still have your natural expectation, but your mind is clear, your body is relaxed, and you use executive functioning. You now have less stress and are better able to deal with anything that may arise.

It's crucial to continually recognize whether or not your I-System is active. For example, someone recklessly cuts in front of you when you're driving. You might think, *He shouldn't drive recklessly; he could have killed me. Is he nuts?* Your hands clench around the steering wheel, you breathe more quickly, your face gets red, and your shoulders go up. You have the telltale signs of an active I-System that's been triggered by the requirement, *People shouldn't drive recklessly.* When the I-System takes control of the natural thought or expectation, *He shouldn't drive recklessly,* it becomes a requirement. Your blood pressure and stress level rise, impairing your ability to drive safely. You are on the verge of road rage (remember Skip, from chapter 1?). Even after the reckless driver has turned off the road, your mind remains cluttered with thoughts, and your body is still tense. Your I-System pours salt on the wound by continuing to spin your thoughts and by tensing your body, creating even more stress and resentment. You could hang on to that anger and ruin your entire day, or even worse, your distress could cause you to have an uncontrollable outburst. It's important to notice that whenever the I-System captures a natural thought or expectation and makes it into a requirement, you become a victim of circumstances because your ability to act appropriately is handicapped. This chapter gives you the tools to quiet your I-System and regain your executive functioning.

UNCOVER REQUIREMENTS

It's time to start mapping your I-System requirements. Remember that the two-part mind-body maps are short written exercises that take only a few minutes. They're vivid pictures of your thoughts and body tension. Every two-part map you create makes you more aware of your requirements, reduces control by your I-System, and helps you to use your executive functioning.

1. This mapping exercise is a powerful way to uncover requirements that sap your ability to live your best life. Do a How My World Should Be map (see the following sample map). Take a few minutes to write around the oval any thoughts that you have about how your everyday world should be; for example, *My partner shouldn't be so critical* or *People should show me respect*. Be specific and work quickly, without editing your thoughts.

HOW MY WORLD SHOULD BE MAP

HOW MY WORLD SHOULD BE

SAMPLE MAP: HOW MY WORLD SHOULD BE

It should be about to do
what I want.

People should understand me.

HOW MY WORLD SHOULD BE

People should show
me respect.

I shouldn't have to work
so hard.

I should be more
relaxed.

Chris should follow
through with his promises.

I should make more money.

My kids shouldn't be so
demanding.

My partner should
trust me.

I should have a great
barbecue grill.

A. Do you think everything on your map will happen? Yes _____ No _____.

B. In this chart, write down each thought and describe your body tension when you realized that it might not happen.

"How My World Should Be" Thought	Body Tension and Location	
Example 1: My partner should trust me.	*Fist clenched, tense jaw*	√
Example 2: I should have a great barbecue grill.	*Minimal body tension*	

C. The body tension you listed is a sign that the thought is a requirement and has activated your I-System. Place a check mark in the third column to indicate that the particular thought is a requirement.

We all have natural thoughts about how the world should be. When your I-System takes hold of your thoughts about how the world should be and you see that this might not happen, your body tenses and your mind gets cluttered. This sets the stage for you to explode in an angry outburst, with your I-System in control of how you behave.

Remember, thoughts that trigger your I-System are requirements. In the previous example, take the thought, *My partner should trust me.* When you have the thought, *My partner doesn't trust me*, your jaw tightens, your fist clenches, and your thoughts spin. This means you have the requirement, *My partner should trust me*, and your requirement is interfering with your relationship. If your I-System hadn't captured that thought, it would have remained a natural expectation, and your executive functioning would have guided your behavior. For the other thought listed as an example (*I should have a great barbecue grill*), you have minimal body tension when reality (same old barbecue grill) doesn't match that thought. In that case, your I-System is not triggered, so the thought *I should have a great barbecue grill* isn't a requirement, it's a natural thought from executive functioning. It means that if you end up with your old grill, you'll still have a relaxed body and a clear mind.

2. Now you'll use the bridging awareness practices you learned in chapter 1 and do a How My World Should Be map again. Before you start writing, listen to any background sounds, experience your body's pressure on your seat, sense your feet on the floor, and feel the pen in your hand. Take your time. Once you feel settled, keep feeling the pen in your hand and start writing about how your world should be. Watch the ink go onto the paper, and listen to any background sounds. For the next few minutes, jot down whatever comes to mind about how the world should be.

HOW MY WORLD SHOULD BE MAP WITH BRIDGING

HOW MY WORLD SHOULD BE

A. What are the differences between this map and the previous map?

_____

_____

B. Do you see that you can face the world as it is, without having the pressure of your I-System, as is shown by the previous map you made? Yes _____ No _____

When something happens in your life (*My partner spent two thousand dollars on a new TV*) that fills your mind with spinning angry thoughts and tenses your body, you know it's your I-System, not your partner, that makes you feel distressed. If you recognize your requirement and tune in to your senses, you will quiet your I-System. Your mind clutter, body tension, and anger will soon reduce so that you can now handle what's happening with a ready, relaxed mind and body.

Whenever you have body tension and mind clutter, it's a sign that one of your I-System requirements is not being fulfilled and that you may be on the edge of an angry outburst. The mapping exercise you just did is about increasing your awareness of your requirements. Notice your signs of an active I-System. For example, maybe your shoulders start to raise, your jaw tenses, you feel overwhelmed, you feel a pain in your neck, you stop hearing the fan, or you slump in your chair. Once you notice a sign, see if you can find the requirement that activated your I-System. When you identify your requirement, you have more control over what's upsetting you. Remember, it is not the situation or another person's behavior that activates your I-System; it's your own requirement.

3. Mull over the upsetting situations you have had in the past few days, and fill out this chart.

Situation	Mind Clutter	Body Tension	Requirement
Boss keeps giving me too many projects.	I can't get it done; I could punch him in the nose.	Jaw tight, fist clenched, foot tapping	I shouldn't be assigned new projects until I finish the last one.
We might have to cancel our vacation, because the kids are sick.	The kids are always sick; I really need this vacation; pisses me off.	Headache, jittery, back tight	The kids shouldn't get sick and ruin my vacation.

Go back over each requirement you listed on the chart. Use your bridging awareness practices and thought labeling, and see if you have less stress and resentment. Using your anger reduction tools puts your natural self back in charge.

An experienced teacher was frustrated when dealing with her large and unruly class, parents who wouldn't cooperate, and new regulations. Feeling stressed out, angry, and at her wit's end, she tried mind-body bridging. She defined her stressors as too few teaching supplies, no district support, and too large of a class size. After recognizing the requirements related to her stressors, she saw another major requirement: *I should be able to handle anything.* Using anger reduction tools, she labeled her thoughts and tuned in to her senses to calm her I-System. She became aware of what she was holding in her hands, the flavors and textures of what she was eating, and her posture while sitting and standing. Her stress and anger levels decreased, and her tolerance increased. She even taught another teacher, who had been disciplined for yelling at students, to use the same techniques with success.

WHAT MAKES ME MAD

The unexpected is just around the corner, filling life with situations that could upset you. Doing mind-body mapping prepares you to face those situations without melting down. In this exercise, the first map leads you to clearly identify the requirements connected to your anger. The second map lets you feel the mind-body shift from an active I-System to an I-System at rest. Mapping reins in your anger and allows you to function in a natural way in executive mode.

1. Do a What Makes Me Mad map. In the center of the oval, write down a current situation that makes you angry. Next, take a couple of minutes to write around the oval any thoughts that come to mind. Work quickly, without editing your thoughts. At the bottom of the map, carefully describe the areas of your body that are tense.

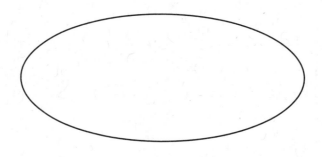

WHAT MAKES ME MAD MAP

Body Tension: _____

_____

What does your map say about how you are approaching the situation?

A. Is your mind cluttered or clear?

_____

Recognizing the start of the tension in your body is a basic first step to managing your anger.

B. Sense what your body feels like when you are beginning to get angry. Note where and how it increases as your anger builds. Describe your buildup of body tension:

_____

_____

_____

C. How would you act in this state?

_____

_____

Your body always gets wound up right before explosive, angry outbursts. No matter what you are thinking, angry outbursts are not possible with a relaxed body.

Recognizing your requirements is crucial to managing your anger. Look at what you wrote in the oval (for example, *Tim lied*) and discover your requirement (*Tim shouldn't lie*). Do the same for each item on your map (*He denies it*) and uncover your requirement (*He should admit it*). This skill of recognizing your requirements can change your entire life.

D. List all the requirements from your map:

_____

_____

_____

_____

When you are not aware of your requirement (*My boss should leave me alone*), your I-System is kept active. You can only have angry outbursts and abuse others with an active I-System. The key to reducing anger is to be aware of your body tension and then recognize your requirement. Once your I-System quiets, your emotions regulate on their own.

2. Use the same situation from the previous map, and do a bridging map using your bridging awareness practices. Write the situation in the oval. Before you start writing, listen to any background sounds, feel your body's pressure on your seat, sense your feet on the floor, and feel the pen in your hand. Take your time. Once you feel settled, keep feeling the pen in your hand, and start writing. Watch the ink go onto the paper, and listen to any background sounds. Take a couple of minutes.

WHAT MAKES ME MAD MAP WITH BRIDGING

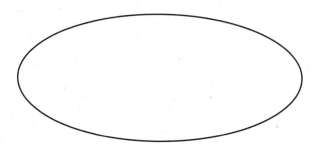

A. Is your mind cluttered or clear?

_____

B. Is your body tense or relaxed?

_____

C. In this mind-body state, how would you act?

_____

D. What are the differences between the two maps?

_____

_____

You don't have to force yourself to act differently. Quieting your I-System with your anger reduction tools allows appropriate actions to flow.

BEFRIEND YOUR BODY

1. Befriending your body is a mind-body bridging tool that is vital for managing your anger. The location, type, amount, and buildup of body tension (clenched fist getting tighter) on the first What Makes Me Mad map are clear-cut signals that when you have tension in that area of your body, your I-System is active. You are now in danger of having an angry outburst where you explode or even abuse others. Go back to the first What Makes Me Mad map and fill out the chart using the items that are filled with the most tension.

What Makes Me Mad	Body Sensation	Behavior	Requirement
My son didn't come home by curfew.	Tight chest; gets hard to breathe	Yelled when he got home	He should be home by curfew.

2. Using your mind-body bridging tools, as you did on the What Make Me Mad Map with Bridging, you experienced a release of body tension. This is your natural state. Go back to the bridging map and fill out the chart below, using the information you listed on that map.

What Makes Me Mad	Body Sensation	State of Mind	Behavior
My son didn't come home by curfew.	Breathing settles down	Worried	Calmly went to his friend's house and brought him home.

Not using your anger reduction tools throughout the day keeps you from being aware of your body's signals. It's important to notice the first signs of body tension, because if you don't, your body tension will increase. Then your mind spins wildly until your body is wound up tight. Your awareness narrows until all you see is a target in front of you, and your mind goes blank as you strike out verbally or physically. It's critical that you recognize the early signs of body tension and start using your anger reduction tools immediately.

3. What anger reduction tools are working best for you? List them:

_____

_____

_____

_____

_____

TRIGGERS

Another important method of improving your ability to manage anger and explosive outbursts is to examine triggers. A *trigger* is an event or thought that activates a requirement, heating up your I-System. Any event is a trigger if, and *only* if, that event violates a requirement. Every coin has two sides, and even when flipped, it's still the same coin. Triggers and requirements are the same way. When you become aware of a trigger, it's important to realize that it's pointing you to the requirement (the other side of the coin). Remember, it's not the event or someone else's behavior that activates the I-System; it's your requirement about that event or behavior.

Al (age fifty, six foot four, and 250 pounds) spent time in prison for assault because he was unable to control his anger. "I would punch first and think later," he said. After his mind-body bridging anger management program, he remarked, "I have the skills to stop my explosive outbursts from developing. Once my jaw tightens and my teeth clench, I immediately listen to the background sounds, feel my feet on the floor, and unwind. My maps show what my triggers are: 'hard eyes looking at me,' 'someone using fancy language and big words,' 'standing too close to me,' 'smiling at me,' and so on. I worked hard to map my requirements. Now I feel like more of a man. I see that my requirements made me feel weak and that I became violent to feel better. My anger reduction tools give me the ability to make better decisions in the heat of the moment."

Life is full of events that upset you, make your I-System active, and create inner distress that drains your emotional resources. When you clearly recognize the triggers (events or thoughts) that switched on your I-System, they will not upset you as much as before. When someone's actions toward you stir up your anger (for example, your mother-in-law insults you), it helps to ask yourself, *What does that trigger behavior look like?* Some answers might be *The pitch of her voice, Her facial expression, Her shaking her finger, The words she uses,* and *Her rigid posture.* Next, look for your hidden requirements that go with each trigger action.

Let's get up close and personal with your triggers. Take a few minutes to do a Triggers map by jotting down what triggers your I-System, such as the way others act or events that happen (for example, *Terry broke his promise, Joe keeps parking in my spot, The plane was late*).

TRIGGERS MAP

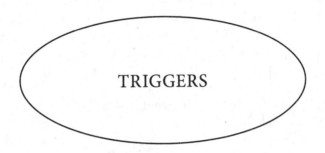

Choose the items from your map that are most likely to make you angry. List these triggers, your associated body tension, and the underlying requirement. Mind-body mapping is always about *your* I-System requirements, not someone else's behavior. Remember that the trigger points to your requirement.

Trigger	Body Tension	Requirement
Terry broke his promise.	*Shoulders raise and then get tighter*	*Terry shouldn't break his promise.*

USE YOUR BODY AS A COMPASS

Throughout the day, be aware of your body tension, especially those areas of your body that were tense on your Triggers map. Although the I-System causes body tension and creates stress in your life, it's no more your enemy than a friend who is giving you vital information. Being aware of the early signs of body tension lets you know when you are heading in the wrong direction (toward an anger buildup, maybe causing you to explode). Use these signals as you would a compass (figure 2.1). When you notice that the I-System is on, know that you are off course. This is when you use your anger reduction tools to quiet your I-System, and your executive functioning will put you back on the right course.

Rob, an auto mechanic, had such a quick temper that he could go from being calm to lashing out with words or fists in a matter of minutes. He told his mind-body bridging group, "I've had a short fuse for as long as I can recall." His Triggers map showed that any actions by others that he felt didn't respect his "picture" of the world would stir up his I-System. Rob first reported that when someone said or did something, he "would get heated up and strike out at them." His What Makes Me Mad map showed the following items: "Thoughts spinning wildly," "Body numb yet full of tension," and "What I'm aware of around me narrows until all I see is a target in front of me."

Because of mapping, Rob came to notice his gradual buildup of body tension that came before each time he exploded in anger: clenched teeth, tight jaw, closed fist, tight muscles all over, and a body that felt ready to explode. By making a daily habit of using bridging awareness practices, he became more sensitive to the early signs of an active I-System (clenched teeth) to remind him to use his anger reduction tools. He said, "I didn't have to wait until my body tension made me shake with anger and it was too late." As he kept doing mind-body maps and using his body as a compass, he had fewer and fewer angry outbursts. Rob told the group, "My flash into anger now takes place in slow motion." As he quieted his body using his anger reduction tools, his thinking cleared. Rob's maps showed him that the trigger set off a requirement that made him feel helpless, weak, and damaged; and his angry outbursts were aimed at fixing that painful state. Once he saw that his I-System was what was making him feel like a victim, he made great headway. He added his anger reduction tools into his daily routine and now, five years later, is still living without anger ruling his life.

Many times your I-System's mind clutter keeps you from knowing how your body feels (body tension), and this sets the stage for angry outbursts. Like Rob, note that when your body reaches a certain level of tension, an angry outburst is bound to happen. Being aware of your buildup of body tension is a crucial mind-body bridging tool. Use your body as a compass (befriend your body) to create mind-body balance in which you are in control of your life. Remember, when your body is tense and your mind cluttered, your I-System is in the driver's seat. To quiet your I-System, use your anger management tools by noting your body tension; recognizing that it's your requirement, not what's happening, that's causing your distress and anger; and then listening to any background sounds, sensing whatever you're touching, and going back to your executive functioning.

Headache   Muscle Aches

Tension   Tightness

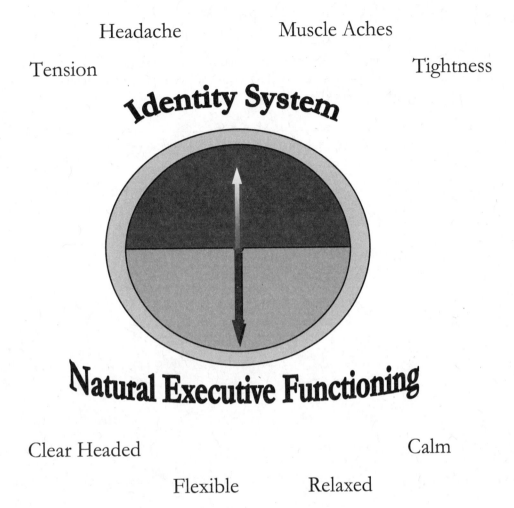

Identity System

Natural Executive Functioning

Clear Headed   Calm

Flexible   Relaxed

Figure 2.1 Use your body as a compass.

A bird that migrates has an inner compass that tells it when it's veering off course on its way home in the spring. When you notice your I-System in action, it becomes your compass, letting you know when you are off course. Being aware calms your I-System and shifts you into natural executive functioning. This puts you on course to deal with your daily life without anger.

ANGER-DISSOLVING MAP

1. When you are upset and it's hard to find the underlying requirements, do a What's on My Mind map. Take a couple of minutes to write whatever pops into your mind around the following oval. Work quickly, without editing your thoughts.

WHAT'S ON MY MIND MAP

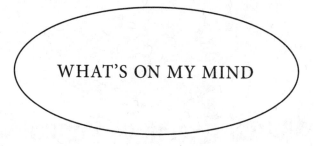

A. Is your mind cluttered or clear?

_____

B. Describe your body tension:

_____

_____

This is a momentary snapshot of what's on your mind. Notice which thoughts are connected to body tension (for example, *My daughter is acting out, I have to choose which bills to pay, My car needs work*). Recognize the requirement in each thought (*My daughter shouldn't act out, I should be able to pay all my bills, My car shouldn't break down*).

C. What are your requirements?

_____

_____

_____

2. Do this map again, this time using your bridging awareness practices. Before you start writing, listen to any background sounds, feel your body's pressure on your seat, sense your feet on the floor, and feel the pen in your hand. Take your time. Once you feel settled, keep feeling the pen in your hand, and start writing. Watch the ink go onto the paper, and listen to any background sounds. For the next few minutes, jot down whatever thoughts pop into your mind.

WHAT'S ON MY MIND WITH BRIDGING

Observe the differences between the two maps:

_____

_____

Remember, thought labeling helps. For example, if you have the thought, *My life could be ruined*, say to yourself, *I'm having the thought, "My life could be ruined."* What is ruining your life right here, right now, isn't losing your job, but the thoughts your I-System has spun about losing the job. You don't have to fix your thoughts, push them away, or force any changes. When the I-System is at rest, your executive functioning natural self will automatically help you make decisions about your course of action without the I-System clouding your mind. During the day, being aware that *A thought is just a thought* is all it takes; then you can return your awareness to the task at hand.

PUTTING IT ALL TOGETHER

By using your mind-body bridging awareness practices, you will get in touch with and express your natural self more and more. In this state, even a slight increase in jaw tension will remind you to use your anger reduction tools, and you'll go back to being your natural self in executive mode.

A contractor was stressed out and constantly angry. He even threw his saw through a wall when it seized up on a job. He was overwhelmed and fearful that his business would fail. After learning mind-body bridging, he used his senses at his job sites by seeing the dust in the air, hearing the construction sounds, and feeling the sensations of his tools in his hands. These bridging awareness practices calmed his I-System so that he could recognize the following requirements:

Customers should pay me as promised.

Customers shouldn't be demanding.

Workers should be reliable.

I should never run out of needed supplies.

"Subs" should always show up.

Workers should never cut corners.

When mapping he reported, "A lightbulb went on. It's not about other people or even about any situation; it's my requirements that are stressing me out! I am not a victim; I'm in control of how I feel and how I act!" He began using his body as a compass to tell him when his I-System was beginning to heat up, and he was able to stay in executive mode more and more. With a quiet I-System, his stress and anger subsided, and he was now able to deal with his job challenges, one problem at a time.

Mind-body bridging is an ongoing practice. Use your anger reduction tools to live every aspect of your life with a calm I-System. Your new tools from this chapter are listed below.

Anger Reduction Tools

➤ Create two-part mind-body maps.

➤ Discover requirements that activate your I-System.

➤ Recognize requirements to quiet your I-System.

➤ Use your body as a compass by befriending your body.

MBB RATING SCALE
IMPROVE EVERYDAY LIFE BY RECOGNIZING REQUIREMENTS

Date: _____

After you use the tools in this chapter for a few days, check the box that best describes your practice for each question: hardly ever, sometimes, usually, or almost always.

How often do you...	Hardly Ever	Sometimes	Usually	Almost Always
Locate and recognize body tension as a sign of an active I-System?				
Use your body as a compass to tell you when your I-System is active?				
Notice the destructive effects that the I-System has on your life?				
Notice that an active I-System is behind your anger?				
Recognize your requirements?				
Catch yourself drifting away from being present in the moment?				
Use bridging awareness practices to quiet your I-System and improve the quality of your life?				
Come to appreciate your life in a different light?				
Do a daily two-part mind-body map?				

When your I-System is active, how do you deal with your anger?

_____

_____

When you are using your anger reduction tools and your I-System is quiet, how do you deal with difficult situations?

_____

_____

What's the most important benefit of doing two-part mind-body maps?

_____

_____

CHAPTER 3

LEARN TO OVERCOME ANGER BY MANAGING TROUBLING THOUGHTS

Principles

The depressor keeps your I-System going with troubling thoughts that make you feel bad about yourself, and sets you up to burst out in anger.

When you defuse the depressor, you shift back into your natural self that functions in executive mode, where you manage your anger.

Mind-Body Language

Powerless self: How you think, feel, see the world, and act when your I-System is active. Life is overwhelming, your executive functioning is impaired, and you struggle vainly to manage your anger.

Depressor: A part of the I-System that takes your natural negative thoughts and self-talk (things you say to yourself), and creates body tension and mind clutter. It makes you feel weak, powerless, and ready to explode.

Storyline: Thoughts that your I-System spins into stories (true or not) that keep your I-System going; they pull you away from the here and now. This can make your anger build up and cause you to make bad decisions.

Defusing the depressor: When you become clearly aware that your negative thoughts are "just thoughts," those thoughts then do not create body tension and mind clutter.

THINKING AND NEGATIVE THOUGHTS

Did you know that from the viewpoint of neuroscience, a thought is just a secretion, a droplet of chemical where two brain cells connect (*synapse*)? Did you know that psychologists and others who study the mind sometimes call thoughts *mind facts*? These mind facts are organized, stored, and used as needed to deal with events as they come up. In this chapter you will learn how your I-System takes hold of your thoughts and makes it hard for you to manage your anger.

It is vital to know how your mind thinks and uses thoughts in order for you to be able to manage your anger. If you have the thought *high*, there must be a *low*; if you think *good*, there must be a *bad*; and the same follows for *happy* and *sad*, *calm* and *angry*, *sick* and *well*, and *young* and *old*. The mind works with both positive and negative thoughts. Most of us struggle over what to do with our negative thoughts. Many people try to use positive affirmations to get rid of or deal with their negative thoughts. We have all tried to fix ourselves with positive affirmations, but when we stop, the negative thoughts come back with a vengeance. So what do we do about negative thoughts? Have you noticed that pushing them away only gives them more energy? For example, try not to think of a red balloon. What are you thinking of? A red balloon! The only time we will get rid of our negative thoughts is when we're brain dead.

So the question remains: What do we do with negative thoughts? The natural self functions in executive mode, creating harmony and balance out of opposite thoughts. For instance, being happy and being sad are emotions that we all have. Your natural self knows how to deal with each. But the I-System has a much different approach; its mission is to keep itself going by grabbing (usually negative) thoughts. The depressor, a part of the I-System, works by taking your negative thoughts and self-talk (things you say to yourself), and creating body tension and mind clutter. It takes a negative thought like *I'm a loser*, *I get no respect*, or *It's no use*, and weaves a story about that thought, filling every cell of your body with negativity and stress. You see yourself as powerless, broken, or ruined, and you have a story to prove it! This state is known as the "powerless self" and is behind all of your unmanaged anger. Because people with problems managing their anger tend to cover up their negative thoughts, it's of upmost importance to be clearly aware of your negative thoughts and feelings about yourself. When you deny or are unaware of your negative self-talk, it makes you feel even more powerless (the powerless self). This is a main reason why you explode into harmful outbursts.

The original question, *What do I do about my negative thoughts?* now becomes *What do I do about my depressor?* The depressor is the doom and gloom of your I-System. It uses the negative self-talk that naturally occurs during the day to make you feel weak and powerless. Today you'll begin to see your negative self-talk for what it is, just thoughts. This is another crucial step in your becoming able to stay in executive mode and avoid angry outbursts.

David had a successful career and a loving, supportive wife, but his negative, self-critical talk was beginning to ruin his life. His negative self-talk included: *I'm not organized enough*; *I should be better*; *I cause my headaches because I can't sleep*; *If I relax, I'll mess up*; *I don't eat right*; and *I'm afraid I'll say the wrong thing*. David's body tension and spinning thoughts were creating insomnia and stomach problems. This negative self-talk was affecting his interactions with others because of his negative focus. All this I-System activity had him angry at himself and depressed. A colleague at work recommended mind-body bridging. After learning the bridging awareness and thought labeling tools, whenever a negative thought would pop up (*I can never get it right*), he would label that thought (*I am having the thought, "I can never get it right"*), come to his senses, and return to what he was doing. David learned about his I-System's depressor and how it captured natural negative thoughts, embedded the negativity into his body, and created spinning thoughts and body tension. David began doing depressor maps and learned how his I-System was making him feel victimized and weak. His outlook began to change as he mapped daily and used his anger reduction tools whenever he recognized that his I-System was active. Now, when a negative thought pops up, after he labels this thought as just a thought, he adds a lighthearted *So what else is new?* and goes about his day.

Try hard to recall your negative self-talk from the past twenty-four hours. On this chart, note your thoughts, the kind of body tension you have, where it's located, and how it builds up (such as jaw is tense and builds until body is heated up). Notice how your negative thoughts are related to your level of body tension.

Negative Self-Talk	Body Tension
I'll never get respect. I should just stop trying.	*Throat tight, building pressure in chest. Getting harder to breathe.*

The secret to gaining control of negative thinking is to know how the depressor works, how it walls you off from your executive mode, and how it makes you prone to exploding in anger. The next maps will give you more tools to unlock your natural self.

KNOW YOUR DEPRESSOR

1. Do a Depressor map. Around the oval, write any negative thoughts and self-talk you have when you're bummed out. If any of the thoughts are positive, see if you can find their negative opposites and jot them down (see the sample map on the next page). Write as much as you can for a couple of minutes.

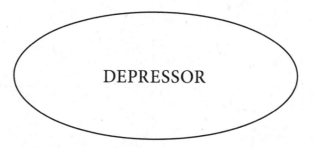

DEPRESSOR MAP

A. Describe your body tension and how it progresses:

_____

_____

B. What's your behavior like when your depressor is active?

_____

_____

C. Describe the impact on your health and quality of life when your depressor is active:

_____

_____

The thoughts on your map are natural thoughts that happen to be negative. The depressor works by grabbing a negative thought and embedding the negativity in your body, which generates even more negative thoughts. This process creates a heavy burden that reduces your ability to manage your anger.

SAMPLE MAP: DEPRESSOR

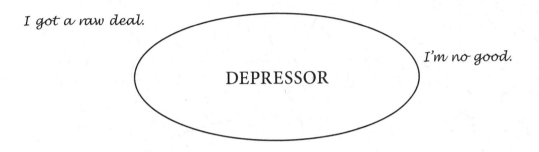

No one understands me.

My family doesn't love me.

I got a raw deal.

DEPRESSOR

I'm no good.

I'm a loser.

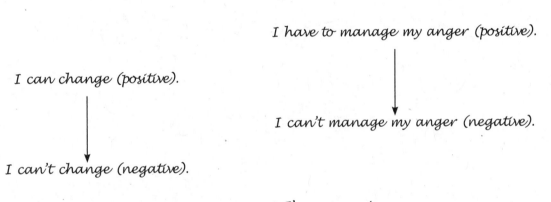

I have to manage my anger (positive).

I can change (positive).

I can't manage my anger (negative).

I can't change (negative).

I'm worn out.

No one has my back.

A. Describe your body tension and how it progresses: *tight shoulders, heavy body. The more negative my thoughts, the more my shoulders raise and the heavier my body feels.*

B. What's your behavior like when your depressor is active? *I first keep to myself, and then I start criticizing and blaming my partner and I end up yelling at everyone.*

2. Time to look at your depressor more closely. From your previous Depressor map, take the thought that troubles you the most by creating a lot of body tension (for example, *No one has my back*), and write it in the following oval. Now, for the next few minutes, write around the oval any thoughts that come to mind. Use phrases or complete sentences like *Nothing I do works*, *My family doesn't love me*, or *I'll never be able to pay the bills*.

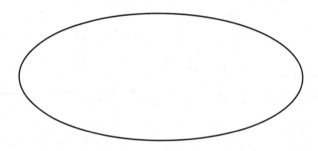

TROUBLING THOUGHT FROM MY DEPRESSOR MAP

Describe your body tension and how it progresses:

_____

_____

The map you just did holds the key to managing your depressor. The thoughts on your map are spun into stories (true or not) by your I-System. Think about the stories that come to mind about your negative thoughts. Remember, these are called "storylines." It's very important to recognize and become aware of how they control you. Storylines are the link between the negative thoughts that pop into your mind and the mind-body distress you experienced on your last two maps. The I-System's spinning storyline takes a natural negative thought and embeds the negativity into every cell of your body, resulting in a condition where angry outbursts and abusive behaviors occur. Storylines keep the I-System going, taking you away from the present moment. Stopping the depressor's storylines keeps negative thoughts from causing an explosive outburst.

3. Use your bridging awareness practices and do the previous map again. Write the same troubling thought in the oval. Before you continue, listen to background sounds, feel your body's pressure on your seat, sense your feet on the floor, and feel the pen in your hand. Take your time. Once you feel settled, keep feeling the pen in your hand and start writing. Watch the ink go onto the paper, and listen to background sounds. Write for a couple of minutes.

TROUBLING THOUGHT FROM MY DEPRESSOR MAP WITH BRIDGING

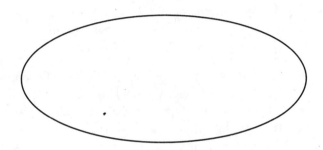

Notice the differences between the two maps:

A. Is your mind cluttered or clear?

_____

B. Is your body tense or relaxed?

_____

C. In this mind-body state, how do you act?

_____

_____

STEPS TO DEFUSE YOUR DEPRESSOR

When you feel down and have body tension, it means your depressor is active. Use the next few tools to defuse your depressor so that your natural self is back in the driver's seat:

1. *Recognizing the depressor:* Know that when your mind has negative thoughts and your body has tension, it's your depressor—not the thoughts, what's happening, or other people—that is causing your distress.

2. *Thought labeling:* Thought labeling is the first tool you use to gain control over troubling thoughts. From one of your maps, choose a thought that still creates body tension. Say slowly to yourself, *I am having the thought* _____ [insert your thought]. Are you sensing a reduction of body tension? Remember, it's your depressor, not the content of your thoughts, that causes your distress.

3. *Bridging awareness practices:* If you still feel body tension after using the steps above, listen to background sounds, and feel your behind on the chair and your feet on the floor. Do you experience a reduction of body tension? If so, you are defusing your depressor.

Diane was forty-five years old, single, lonely, and unhappy. She had a lifelong problem with anger. She recalled that in her teens, when she was angry with her parents, she would rebel, take drugs, and sleep around. Even though she wasn't happy with her behavior, she did it anyway to "get even with them." As an adult, her angry outbursts caused her to lose a good job when she got furious with her boss, screamed at him, and ran out of the office while knocking things off coworkers' desks. When a neighbor didn't act as Diane wanted, Diane would yell, point a finger at the person, and call out whatever dirty names she could think of. After failing to make progress in a number of therapies, she began seeing a mind-body bridging therapist. At first, if the group didn't go the way she wanted, Diane would get red in the face, jump up, cuss, and slam the door as she left the group. Her mind-body mapping helped her recognize her requirements, and see that her depressor made her feel so helpless and weak that, as she put it, "My only escape was rage." Soon, Diane's actions in the group and daily interactions with others changed in a way that everyone noticed. Using her thought labeling and bridging awareness practices let Diane keep her natural self in the driver's seat in the heat of the moment. Diane was even able to be in a relationship with her parents again, whom she had not seen or talked to for fifteen years.

STORYLINE AWARENESS SETS YOU FREE

Another powerful tool for reducing your anger is storyline awareness. Remember, storylines are thoughts spun into stories that keep your I-System active. Storylines aren't just stories; they have a harmful physical effect on your body, and cloud your mind. The negative storylines tend to define us, and the positive ones tend to confine us. All storylines keep you living in the past or dreaming of the future. This takes you away from being present in the moment and handling what's happening right now with your natural self in charge. Storyline awareness is simply noticing the storyline, seeing the damage it's doing, and letting your awareness stop the story. Your executive functioning is restored without your even trying.

Andy, age twenty-one, was newly married. He thought his new bride was cheating on him, which often led to arguments and, later, violence in the form of his pushing, shoving, and slapping her. Andy was ordered by the court to attend domestic violence classes. After a few sessions of mind-body bridging, Andy learned about storylines and how the depressor creates them by hooking his natural negative thoughts and spinning stories, often adding things that aren't true or deleting things that he would rather not face. Andy did a Troubling Thought from My Depressor map and was able to see the storylines that he was playing when he and his spouse would argue; for example, storylines like *She isn't paying attention to me, so she must have someone else*; *She said hi to that guy, so they must have something going on*; and *She keeps getting texts from that guy at work, so he must be hitting on her*. Every time he played these stories, true or not, they filled his body with tension and his mind with clutter, and he would often fly into a rage. Once he became aware of these storylines, Andy was able to quiet his I-System and see things for what they were. As a result, he found that he could better manage his feelings about what was or wasn't happening. Andy realized that his wife wasn't cheating on him, and he was able to tolerate her talking with other men, without getting suspicious or jealous.

By using your storyline awareness tool (just being aware of the storyline) during the day, you'll see how much of your time storylines swallow up. You don't need to push the story away; you just need to become aware of it. Your awareness dissolves the storyline and will even help you sleep better at night.

Tim had an active imagination, and whenever his wife, Sheri, was late, he would immediately start running stories in his mind about what she was doing or what happened to her. His thoughts would start out rather benign. When she was late coming home from work and couldn't be reached on her cell phone, he would think she was in an important meeting and couldn't break free to call him. With a clenched jaw, he began embellishing his thoughts: *She could take a bathroom break and call me. She is being really inconsiderate. What is she doing that she doesn't want me to know about?* By this time his depressor was in full gear and his body even tighter, and as he paced the floor, he would continue with, *Why is she doing this to me?* In this painful state, he was unable to think about anything else. When Sheri would finally get home, Tim would yell and scream at her, demanding, "Why have you put me through this?" Although Sheri loved Tim, enough was finally enough. It was anger management class, or she would divorce him. Tim found that his bridging awareness practices and thought labeling would, as he put it, "ground me and settle down my racing thoughts." After mapping Tim realized that it was *his* thoughts and storylines, not Sheri's behavior, that were causing his meltdowns. By focusing on the background sounds, labeling his thoughts, and being keenly aware of his storylines, he reported, "My imagination became just my imagination. Now when Sheri is late, I don't have to try to create reasons why she's late. I recognize my storylines, defuse my depressor, and go back to what I was doing."

Thinking back over the past week, observe how your I-System created negative storylines filled with tension. Note the body tension that came with that, and find your hidden requirement. Fill out the chart below:

Situation	Negative Storylines	Body Tension	Requirement
He didn't ask me for a date.	*He thinks I'm not good enough for him.*	*Band around my head, jaw tight, grinding my teeth*	*He should ask me for a date.*
She criticized me.	*I'm just a victim; she knows how it hurts me.*	*Tight fist*	*She shouldn't criticize me.*

Start mulling over one of your most distressing storylines and try to keep it going. Now, become aware of background sounds. While continuing to listen to those sounds, observe how your storyline unfolds. Is the storyline running out of gas? Continuing to use your bridging awareness practices weakens your storylines.

MANAGE YOUR "WHAT IFS"

1. The following maps take a look at those "what ifs" that create distress whenever you think about them or even try to not think about them. Do a What If map. Take a couple of minutes to write around the oval any "what if" thoughts that come to mind about important situations in your life that may have a negative outcome (see the sample map on the following page). Work quickly, without editing your thoughts.

WHAT IF MAP

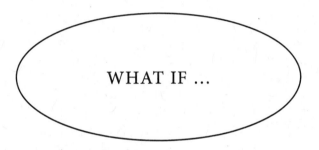

A. Describe your body tension and how it progresses:

_____

_____

B. List your depressors and storylines:

_____

_____

C. List your requirements:

_____

_____

D. In this mind-body state, how do you act?

_____

SAMPLE MAP: WHAT IF

... I really hurt her next time?

... I lose my house?

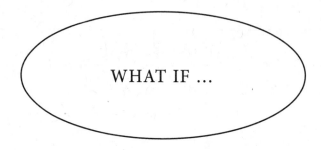

WHAT IF ...

... I get another DUI?

... my daughter doesn't get better grades?

... he finds out the truth?

... my husband doesn't stop smoking?

... my mother doesn't recover from surgery?

... I can't find a job that pays better?

... she doesn't love me?

... he keeps beating me?

... my partner is having an affair?

... I can't get a good night's sleep?

A. Describe your body tension and how it gets worse: *starts with a knot in my stomach, but the more I go over the "what ifs," the more my whole body tenses up and I end up with a headache.*

2. Use your bridging awareness practices and do the map again. Before you begin to write, listen to background sounds, feel your body's pressure on your seat, sense your feet on the floor, and feel the pen in your hand. Take your time. Once you feel settled, keep feeling the pen in your hand and start writing. Watch the ink go onto the paper, and listen to background sounds. Write for a couple of minutes.

WHAT IF MAP WITH BRIDGING

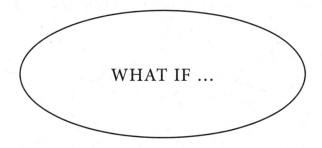

Notice the differences between the two maps:

A. Is your mind cluttered or clear?

_____

B. Is your body tense or relaxed?

_____

C. In this mind-body state, how do you act?

_____

_____

D. Are you more apt to successfully manage your anger in this mind-body state than on the previous map? Yes _____ No _____

RESOLVE YOUR MOST DISTRESSING "WHAT IF"

1. Most of us have an underlying "what if" that makes us sick to our stomachs whenever we think about it (*What if I really hurt her? What if I can't control my anger?*). Do another map using any "what if" that creates body tension and could lead to an angry outburst. Write the item in the oval. Next, take a couple of minutes to write around the oval any thoughts that come to mind. Work quickly, without editing your thoughts.

MOST DISTRESSING WHAT IF MAP

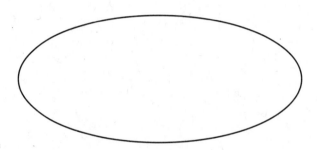

A. Describe your body tension and how it progresses:

_____

_____

B. List your depressors and storylines:

_____

_____

C. List your requirements:

_____

_____

D. In this mind-body state, how likely are you to have an angry outburst?

_____

2. Using your bridging awareness practices, do the previous map again. Write the same troubling item in the oval. Before you continue, listen to background sounds, feel your body's pressure on your seat, sense your feet on the floor, and feel the pen in your hand. Take your time. Once you feel settled, keep feeling the pen in your hand and start writing. Watch the ink go onto the paper, and listen to background sounds. Write for a couple of minutes.

MOST DISTRESSING WHAT IF MAP WITH BRIDGING

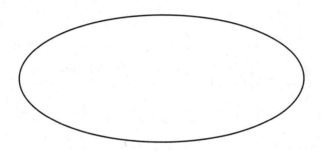

Notice the differences between the two maps:

A. Is your mind cluttered or clear?

_____

B. Is your body tense or relaxed?

_____

C. In this mind-body state, how likely are you to have an angry outburst?

_____

KEY QUESTIONS TO HELP YOU OVERCOME NEGATIVE THOUGHTS

Answer the following questions when your negative thoughts are getting you down:

1. What are the signals that your depressor is active (*heavy body, knot in stomach, thoughts that I'm not good enough*)?

    _____

2. What is your behavior like when your depressor gets you down (*get angry, become irritable, want to be left alone, drink too much, punch the wall, explode, feel bad, and try to apologize*)?

    _____

    _____

3. How is the depressor getting in the way of your executive functioning (*I'm not making good decisions, My parenting is inconsistent, I lose my temper, I feel enormous pressure to fix how I feel*)?

    _____

    _____

4. Do you experience yourself as losing control of your life? Yes _____ No _____
    How so?

    _____

5. What are your storylines (*No matter how hard I work, nothing seems to go my way*)?

    _____

    _____

    _____

6. Are these thoughts and storylines creating who you are? Yes _____ No _____
    How so?

    _____

7. What are your requirements (*My life should be easier, Things should go my way*)?

    _____

    _____

Your depressor interferes with your natural self in executive mode, and makes you see yourself as weak and powerless. This sets the stage for your angry outbursts.

PUTTING IT ALL TOGETHER

Kris, a twenty-one-year-old mother of one, was depressed and discouraged with life, and would often drink away her woes. When she was drunk, she would argue with her live-in boyfriend and would often get to the point where she raged, threw things, and put her young child at risk. After one such time, she was arrested and later ordered by the court to attend substance abuse treatment and classes in domestic violence. During session three of her mind-body bridging program, Kris learned about her depressor and how it hooks her negative thoughts into storylines. Her storylines filled her body with tension and her mind with spinning thoughts about what a loser she was: *I am a terrible mother. I have nothing to live for. My boyfriend thinks I'm unattractive. What's the use?* After doing a depressor map every day for a week, Kris was able to recognize her depressor, find her underlying requirements, and know that her negative thoughts were just thoughts. She was also able to spot her storylines and see that they were often playing just prior to her wanting to go get drunk and numb out. This recognition helped Kris to quiet her I-System and choose to stop drinking, and later, her violent behavior stopped. She was also able to know that her negative thoughts were just natural negative thoughts, and that she had a choice whether or not to buy into them. Kris also began to feel better about herself. Her relationships with her child and her boyfriend improved greatly.

Let's look at the anger reduction tools Kris used to defuse her depressor:

1. She recognized that it was her depressor, not her negative thoughts, overwhelming her.

2. She used thought labeling to get control of her negative thoughts.

3. She became aware that the spin of her storylines made her feel so bad about herself that it drove her to drink and become violent.

4. She used her anger reduction tools to calm her I-System and go back to her natural self, which functioned in executive mode.

Below are the three new tools discussed in this chapter. Use them with the tools you learned in the previous two chapters to defuse your depressor and access your natural self.

Anger Reduction Tools

➤ Uncover your negative thoughts and feelings about yourself.

➤ Recognize the depressor's activity.

➤ Become aware of your storyline.

➤ Defuse the depressor.

MBB RATING SCALE

LEARN TO OVERCOME ANGER BY MANAGING TROUBLING THOUGHTS

Date: _____

After using the tools in this chapter for a few days, check the box that best describes your practice: hardly ever, sometimes, usually, almost always.

How often do you...	Hardly Ever	Sometimes	Usually	Almost Always
Notice negative self-talk and body tension as a sign of the depressor?				
Notice that your depressor is running wild and making you feel weak and powerless?				
Experience that the powerless self comes from your I-System?				
Recognize that an active depressor sets the stage for angry outbursts?				
Defuse your depressor by staying aware of what it is doing and using thought labeling?				
Recognize storylines?				
Recognize natural executive functioning when your I-System is quiet?				

List the body tension that comes along with the depressor and how it progresses:

_____

_____

List the themes of two storylines:

_____

_____

List two behaviors that are connected with the depressor:

_____

_____

What's it like to defuse your depressor and live with a quiet I-System?

_____

_____

CHAPTER 4

BE STRONG WITHOUT ANGER

Principles

· The I-System's fixer is the driving force behind your angry outbursts.

· When you defuse the fixer, you quickly reduce your anger. Then you can handle daily life from a place of inner strength and executive functioning.

Mind-Body Language

Fixer: The depressor's partner that pushes you with overactive, never-ending thoughts of how to fix yourself and the world. All your angry and destructive outbursts are fixer driven.

Defusing the fixer: When you become clearly aware (at the time you are doing something) that your fixer is active and use your anger reduction tools, you take away the fixer's power. Right away, you feel a shift from a stressful, angry state to one with a ready and relaxed mind and body. You can now calmly take care of yourself and whatever you have to do in executive mode.

Depressor/fixer cycle: These I-System partners create a vicious cycle, keep the I-System going and going, and cause your angry and harmful actions.

THE HIDDEN ENEMY WITHIN: THE FIXER

Requirements, depressors, and fixers are the three major parts of the I-System. Requirements are the I-System's rules about how you and the world should be. When a requirement is broken, this switches on the I-System. Then the depressor and fixer jump in, interact with each other, and keep the I-System going. In this chapter we will focus on the fixer. The fixer is the depressor's lifelong, faithful partner that drives you to repair, fix, or get even for the negative, painful state the depressor has caused. The fixer starts from the false belief (caused by the depressor) that you are broken, tries to fix you, and works by making you believe it's really helping you. Your fixer pressures you into feeling the urgent need to take action. When it's active, enough will never be enough. You can recognize the fixer when you notice your increased body tension and a mind full of thoughts like *Get even*, *Be stronger*, *Be angry*, or *Get away*. No matter what you do, the depressor will jump in with thoughts like *Not good enough* and *Weak and powerless*, pushing your fixer to do even more. The depressor and fixer work with each other (depressor/fixer cycle). This cycle keeps the I-System going, and leads to the powerless self and to angry, violent actions.

Jed was a popular restaurant owner who enjoyed success. He never behaved in an angry and aggressive way until his teenage son, Joey, became definat toward him. Feeling helpless, Jed had a harder and harder time handling his son's actions without getting angry. Once, when Joey would not finish raking leaves, Jed shocked himself when, in anger, he broke the rake in half. Even a class in parenting strategies didn't help him parent without having angry outbursts. When he realized his anger was a big problem, Jed signed up for a mind-body bridging group and began using anger reduction tools. Jed quickly recognized that his requirements for Joey (*He should be on time for meals*, *He should do his homework*, *He should do his chores*) kept his I-System heated up. His Depressor map had items like *I'm a bad father*, *I can't control my son*, and *I'm weak*. Jed came to see that his depressor made him feel so helpless that his fixer took control and was trying to fix what was happening with more rules and demands. When those didn't work either, Jed would yell and do aggressive things like breaking the rake. He remarked, "I'm about one step away from hitting my son."

After he did other two-part requirement and fixer maps in this book, Jed was able to see his depressor/fixer cycle, quiet his I-System, and find sensible and calmer ways to parent. He shared with the group that without bridging, it didn't matter what he knew about good parenting, because his requirements (*My son should be a success*, *My son should learn the value of hard work*) were making his I-System active. Next his fixer would drive him to become angry and aggressive, leaving his parenting skills of being smart and patient hidden in the fog of his I-System. Jed's relationship with his son got better as he saw his fixer in action and learned that he could be a strong father without anger. Joey's sense of responsibility (although not perfect) began to build. More importantly, Jed was building a healthy father-son relationship.

Your actions during the day are either driven by the fixer or are executive functioning. All your angry outbursts are driven by the fixer. While you are doing something, try to see the difference between the two; see your I-System's fixer in action, and be strong without anger. Your natural self in executive mode is now in charge, and you can better manage angry outbursts.

MEET YOUR FIXER

1. It's natural to want to improve our lives and reach our goals, so it's critical to recognize when the fixer is in control. The following fixer map is really going to surprise you. Jot down around the oval the thoughts that come up about "How I Am Going to Improve My Life." Work quickly for a couple of minutes, without editing your thoughts.

HOW I AM GOING TO IMPROVE MY LIFE MAP

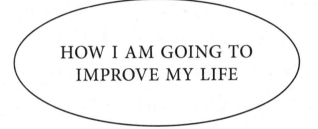

    A. Looking at your map overall, how do you feel?
        Calm _____ Tense _____ Overwhelmed _____

    B. Consider each item on your map and figure how much body tension you have when you think about going for this self-improvement goal. Next to each item on your map, note your level of body tension, using one of these symbols: Ø for no body tension, + for mild, ++ for moderate, or +++ for severe. It may help to see the sample map at the end of the exercise.

    The statements on your map may be either fixer thoughts from an active I-System or natural thoughts from executive functioning. The thoughts that come with body tension are fixer thoughts from your I-System, and the thoughts with no body tension are from executive functioning. Your challenge is telling the difference between the two. Body tension that comes with thoughts means your I-System is active. The fixer brings a mental urgency, creating extra pressure for you to act. Remember, executive functioning is how you think, feel, see the world, and act when your I-System is quiet. When you are in executive-functioning mode and don't reach a goal, you're naturally disappointed. But when you don't reach a fixer goal, you feel devastated; your mind spins with angry thoughts, and your body is tense. For all your efforts and good intentions to succeed, it's important to know which of your daily activities the fixer is capturing.

C. Again, look over each item on your map and imagine that you're not going to reach that goal. Describe what happens to your body tension. Note your angry or irritating thoughts:

_____

_____

D. If you now feel body tension and mind clutter for items that were previously at level Ø, those items have become fixer thoughts. List your fixer thoughts from this map:

_____

_____

_____

E. List your thoughts on this map that are from executive functioning (tension free):

_____

_____

2. It's important to compare the Depressor map in chapter 3 (the first map in that chapter) to this Fixer map titled "How I Am Going to Improve My Life":

A. Which map has the higher overall energy levels (makes you feel better)?
Depressor map _____ Fixer map _____

The higher levels of energy that come with the fixer (and make you feel better) aren't unusual. This higher endorphin level can keep you from recognizing your fixer, because you feel good about the thoughts. When it is active, the fixer clouds your judgment and affects your actions. Thoughts on this map that are driven by the fixer (*Impress my boss with my abilities, Be a better parent*) can set you up to overwork, seek risky thrills, or do addictions or angry and harmful actions.

B. Your body is always giving you helpful information. Note the differences in location, quality, and intensity of the body tension that comes with the thoughts on the Depressor and Fixer maps (for example, *My body tension on the Depressor map was located around my gut, and my body felt heavy and unresponsive; on my Fixer map, my body tension is around my chest and head, and there's a jittery feeling*).

_____

_____

The intensity of your body tension and the driving pressure of your storylines are important signs that the fixer is active. Storylines are a sign that your fixer is limiting your ability to deal with what's happening here and now.

SAMPLE MAP: HOW I AM GOING TO IMPROVE MY LIFE

Be more creative. Ø

Won't let anyone take advantage
of me. ++

HOW I AM GOING TO
IMPROVE MY LIFE

Be more in control. +++

Be a better parent. +++

Eat less and healthier. +++

Go to the gym four
times a week. ++

Manage my money more wisely. +

Create better teamwork
through activities. Ø

Have more free time. +++

Get rid of my anger. +++

Fixer thoughts come with body tension when you think about trying to reach your goals or imagine that you won't reach your goals (for example, *Be a better parent, Eat less and healthier, Won't let anyone take advantage of me, Be more in control, Get rid of my anger, Go to the gym four times a week, Have more free time*). Also note any thoughts from natural functioning (without body tension, marked Ø; for example, *Be more creative* and *Create better teamwork through activities*).

THE MASKS OF THE FIXER

The mask of the fixer takes many forms. For instance, Randy was always angry because, as he said, "Things never go my way." Mari was on an endless merry-go-round that left her feeling exhausted and irritated from being so busy meeting her family's needs. Connie drove herself so hard at work that she needed medicine to lower her blood pressure. Ray tried so hard to be a "good husband" that his wife almost left him. Larry's stressors so overwhelmed him that he tried to "fix" himself with a bottle of whiskey a day. Lyn loved driving very fast, because it made her feel alive and free. Alex was so competitive that no win was ever enough, and he was even driven to compete with his teenage son. Judi was so obsessed with staying young that it affected her relationship with her teenage daughter.

The fixer activates mental pressure that urges you to act. It drives your actions or leaves you feeling resentful and angry. Be aware of the way your fixer frames the demand. The fixer traps you into thinking, *I need to, I have to, I must,* or *I will.* When your I-System is switched on and the fixer is in the driver's seat, it can drive activities that are difficult for you to control: angry and destructive behavior, overeating, drinking too much, taking substances, lying, and taking shortcuts. The fixer clouds your judgment, pushing you to do what relieves your tension or provides instant pleasure. At the time, you may feel you made the right choice, but later you're sorry. You ignored the law of cause and effect, because your fixer kept you unaware of the consequences of your choice. Whenever your fixer is active, you experience body tension, storylines, and mental pressure. Notice how your fixer pushes your behavior.

The fixer will mask itself as the great savior in your life. At first the fixer seems to improve your life and seems helpful. Remember, the fixer's real job is to fix how the depressor makes you feel and to keep the I-System going. This strengthens the powerless self. At times, the fixer uses positive thoughts like *Be in control, Exercise more, Eat better, Sleep better, Work harder, Enjoy life,* or *Be a better parent,* which hide the underlying depressor thoughts: *I'm not in control, I'm fat, I eat wrong, I don't take care of myself, I'm lazy, I don't deserve to have fun,* or *I'm a bad parent.* These hidden depressor thoughts make you feel so awful that you soon have fixer thoughts like *Pass everyone on the road, Punch out that son of a bitch,* and *Have that bottle of wine.*

Never underestimate the *urgency* the fixer creates when it tries to fix the powerless self. Since these fixer thoughts come with mental and physical pressure, they drive fixer activities, like angry outbursts and abuse. For example, the urge to get angry, overeat, drink, or take drugs is the fixer trying to fix how your depressor makes you feel. However, after you do the fixer driven activity, your depressor creates more negative feelings, and this pushes the fixer back into action. This creates a stressful yo-yo effect (depressor/fixer/depressor/fixer…). All of this builds so much tension and mental turmoil that it clouds your ability to see the effects of your actions. The fixer can also disguise itself as a helper by pushing you to diet, stop getting angry, stop drinking, or stop taking drugs. Even when these attempts seem positive, your success doesn't often last very long, because they are carried out with an active I-System and not by the natural self in executive mode. To break this cycle, become actively aware of the fixer's mental and physical pressure that drives your activity, and recognize your depressor, which lies beneath the surface.

YOUR FIXER HAS AN UNDERLYING DEPRESSOR

1. Every fixer has an embedded depressor that drives it. Look again at the fixer map, "How I Am Going to Improve My Life." Write down your embedded depressor thoughts under the fixer thoughts. See the following sample map.

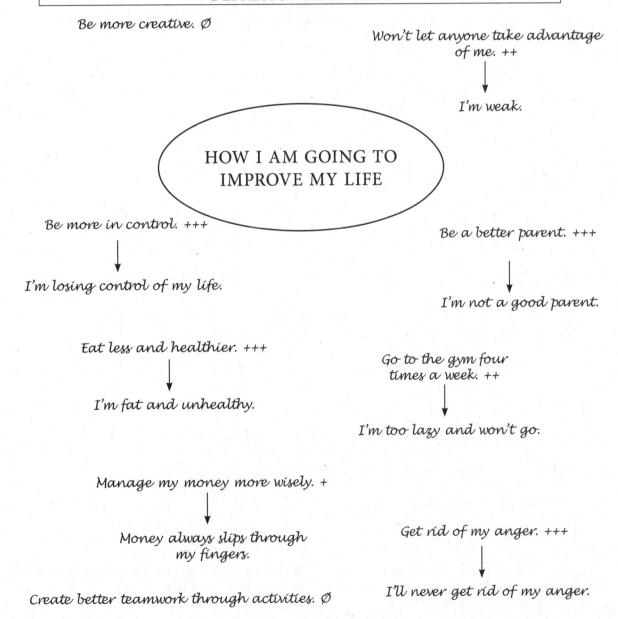

SAMPLE MAP: HOW I AM GOING TO IMPROVE MY LIFE WITH DEPRESSOR THOUGHTS

Be more creative. Ø

Won't let anyone take advantage of me. ++

I'm weak.

HOW I AM GOING TO IMPROVE MY LIFE

Be more in control. +++

I'm losing control of my life.

Be a better parent. +++

I'm not a good parent.

Eat less and healthier. +++

I'm fat and unhealthy.

Go to the gym four times a week. ++

I'm too lazy and won't go.

Manage my money more wisely. +

Money always slips through my fingers.

Create better teamwork through activities. Ø

Get rid of my anger. +++

I'll never get rid of my anger.

2. Think about last weekend. The fixer is always active when you attempt to escape from how the depressor makes you feel. Below, note any of your activities that created mental or physical pressure (fixer activity). Can you find the embedded depressor activity? Note your body tension with Ø for none, + for mild, ++ for moderate, or +++ for severe.

Fixer Driven Behavior	Tension Level	Depressor Thought	Storyline
Threw my cell phone.	+	I'm a victim.	Cell service is no good.
Drank too much.	+++	Nothing goes right.	I deserve to relax.
Threw a vase at my partner.	+++	I feel helpless, unloved.	He asked for it.
Maxed out my credit card.	++	I feel empty, deprived.	It's shopping therapy.
Played violent computer games.	++	I'm tense, depressed.	It feels great to blow stuff up.
Refused to take my meds.	+	I'm sick of medication.	I really don't need it.

A. When your fixer was active, what were the consequences of your behavior (Outcomes for *Drank too much*: *Got sick, missed work, spent my rent money*)?

_____

_____

_____

B. What was the common underlying requirement you were trying to meet?

_____

_____

To stop the depressor/fixer cycle and reduce the anger in your life, you need to recognize and defuse the depressor that lies beneath the surface. With a quiet I-System, your natural self will be in charge of your work, relationships, and play.

THE DANCE OF THE DEPRESSOR/FIXER

Not only does the depressor/fixer cycle cause sleepless nights, addictions, burnout, and poor performance, and harm to your relationships, it's also the main cause of your angry and harmful actions. When you see your depressor/fixer cycle, you build strength without anger.

Fred did not seem to be angry, but his family and friends had trouble with his strong opinions and his stubborn and resistant nature. Because he was very bright (earned a PhD in computer science), he was a rising star in his company, until it became clear to upper management that he wasn't a team player. Fred made it clear to his mind-body bridging therapist that he firmly believed the company was mistaken and that they couldn't stand to hear the truth. At first he resisted mind-body bridging. But then he learned about the depressor/fixer cycle, and started to map more. To his great surprise, he came to realize that his behavior was driven by the fixer, and always came up when something or someone made him feel vulnerable. His two-part maps gave him confidence that his natural self, functioning in executive mode, meant that he didn't need his fixer to protect him. He remarked, "Knowing about my fixer opened me up to be a better team player."

When the I-System is active, it causes your behavior to be fixer driven. When your behavior is angry, controlling, or aggressive, your fixer is in the driver's seat. When you feel weak and out of control, the depressor is in the driver's seat. The depressor and fixer have an interesting relationship. You automatically strengthen one when you push away, reject, or deny the other. For example, when you don't recognize the passive, weak, helpless thoughts the depressor has captured, the fixer becomes more energized and can result in controlling and aggressive behaviors. When you fail to recognize or when you deny your assertive and controlling thoughts that have been grabbed by the fixer, this results in more depressor thoughts and body tension. When the I-System is quiet, this means your depressor and fixer are no longer active, and your natural self is in the driver's seat.

Cody, a thirty-five-year-old father of three with a struggling marriage, had just lost his business. He was depressed, discouraged, and angry, and his best efforts to fix his difficult situation all seemed to fail. Cody was often on edge, and the most trivial things seemed to set him off. He would go into a rage, sometimes knocking holes in the walls of his home with his fist, frightening his family. After one such incident, the neighbors called the police. He was arrested and ordered by the court to attend anger management classes. Angry and bitter, Cody protested that he had the right to knock holes in his own walls if he wanted.

After several sessions of mind-body bridging anger management classes and learning to calm his I-System with his anger reduction tools, Cody's anger began to abate. His real breakthrough came when he learned about his fixer trying to fix his depressor. Because his I-System convinced him that he was helpless and damaged, his fixer would respond with anger and rage. As Cody worked on seeing his depressor/fixer cycle, something happened. He realized that it was his fixer in control when he would smash holes in the walls. This shifted his entire attitude about his behavior. Where, once, he felt justified in his actions, he now felt his previous actions to be wrong. Using all of his anger reduction tools in his daily life, Cody became patient and flexible, and gained the ability to deal with life's situations with a relaxed body and mind.

WHY YOUR TO-DOS ARE MAKING YOU ANGRY

You can get frustrated as you think about the never-ending list of annoying to-dos. The next two-part map shows you how your fixer is making it harder to get through your list.

1. Around the oval, jot down all the things you need to get done over the next few days that could be frustrating to you. Write for a couple of minutes, without editing your thoughts. The following sample map may be helpful.

TO-DO MAP

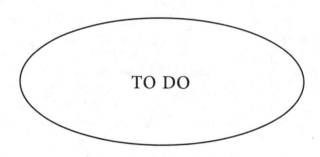

TO DO

A. Next to each item on your map, note your level of body tension, using one of these symbols: Ø for no body tension, + for mild, ++ for moderate, or +++ for severe. It may help to see the sample map that follows. Those items with body tension are fixers.

B. List the storylines associated with the three fixers with the most body tension:

_____

_____

_____

SAMPLE MAP: TO DO

Find another route around
the construction. Ø

Finalize plans for the new project
at work. ++

TO DO

Visit my in-laws. +++

Pay my bills. ++

Take the kids to the dentist. ++

Go to the parent-teacher
conference. +++

Buy an inexpensive
birthday present. +

Get car serviced. +

Call Mom. +++

Find time for a run. +

Sample storylines:

Call Mom: *I should call her now. Maybe she'll leave me alone. Knowing her, she'll call me all weekend, wanting me to drive her around. Why does this happen every weekend?*

Go to the parent-teacher conference: *Charlie won't do his homework, and I can't do anything about it. He lies about his grades. I'm pissed. The teacher should do a better job.*

Finalize plans for the new project at work: *I need to do more work at home, or it won't be done right. My boss demands too much from me. He's a jackass. If only I could give him a piece of my mind.*

2. Now do the map again, this time using your bridging awareness practices, and see what happens. Before you start writing, listen to background sounds, feel your body's pressure on your seat, sense your feet on the floor, and feel the pen in your hand. Take your time. Once you're settled, keep feeling the pen in your hand, and start writing. Scatter your thoughts around the oval. Watch the ink go onto the paper, and listen to background sounds. Write for a couple of minutes.

TO-DO MAP WITH BRIDGING

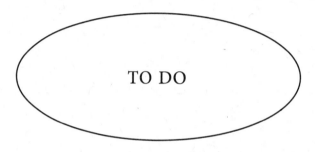

A. Compare the two maps. What do you notice?

_____

B. In this mind-body state, how do you experience your to-do list?

_____

_____

The release of body tension, and the reduced mind clutter and sense of urgency, mean that you have shifted into executive functioning. You learned that it was the depressor/fixer cycle, with its related storylines, that made you feel overwhelmed and angry, not what you have to do. Without the I-System adding any stress or taking away any power, you manage the things you have to do much better and more naturally.

Now that you have calmed your I-System and freed yourself from its burden, it's time for you to take care of your to-do list with your natural self in charge.

UNMASKING YOUR FIXER

Your days are filled with activities. Many of them may be free of anger (for example, brushing your teeth, playing with your dog, and getting recognized for a job well done). Others (for example, rushing to an appointment or meeting, pushing yourself to meet a deadline, dealing with a never-ending list of demands for your time) could well come with body tension and storylines (frustrated and angry self-talk). When you unmask the fixer, your activities that were filled with tension are now tension free and are carried out with a quiet I-System.

Think back over the last twenty-four hours and notice any specific body tension, mental pressure, or feelings of being driven. That's your fixer in action. See if you can find the different characteristics of body tension (location, type, or both) that come with your fixer.

Activity	Body Tension and Location	Storyline	Fixer-Driven Behavior
Rushing to work	*Tense neck, chest pressure*	*My boss has it in for me! The traffic lights are timed all wrong.*	*Drive fast and go through yellow lights.*

The fixer may also be involved when you can't seem to move on from an issue. Maybe at night, when you're trying to sleep, a situation where you thought someone was disrespectful plays over and over in your mind. Your I-System's fixer is in high gear, interfering with your sleep as you try to figure out how to fix the situation or get back at the person. Doing a two-part What's on My Mind map before bed is very helpful. Remember to also use bridging awareness practices and thought labeling to get a good night's sleep. Quality sleep is your number one way to revitalize, whereas poor sleep can cause you to start the next day grumpy or angry.

WHAT YOU MOST WANT TO AVOID

1. Think about something important that you don't want to do (*Visit my mother-in-law* or *Routinely exercise*). Write it in the oval. For several minutes, jot down around the oval any thoughts that come up about that situation. The following sample map may be helpful.

WHAT I DON'T LIKE TO DO MOST MAP

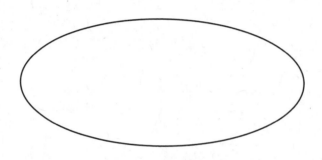

A. Next to each item on your map, note your level of body tension, using one of these symbols: Ø for no body tension, + for mild, ++ for moderate, or +++ for severe. It may help to see the sample map that follows.

SAMPLE MAP: WHAT I DON'T LIKE TO DO MOST

She never sees me as good enough for her family. +++

She is a good cook. Ø

VISIT MY MOTHER-IN-LAW

She won't stop talking and never listens. ++

She criticizes me. +++

I shouldn't have to go there. +++

She drives me nuts. +

I feel like a target. +++

She's always complaining about something. ++

She always has a to-do list for me. +

I freeze up and shake with anger when she laughs at me. +++

My spouse and I always have a fight after visiting. +++

Just thinking about her makes me angry. +++

B. From the map you just did, you can see step-by-step how the I-System takes an event, creates inner distress, and drives your fixer behavior. Below, list the three map items with the most body tension and then follow the instructions in the chart.

Map Item With Most Body Tension	Requirement: How you think you or the other person should act	Depressor Thought: While thinking about the map item, list your negative thoughts.	Depressor Body Sensation: What are your negative body sensations?	Fixer Thought: How are you going to fix how the depressor makes you feel?	Fixer Body Sensation: What does your body feel like with the fixer active?	Fixer Behavior: What would you like to do about it?
She criticizes me.	She shouldn't criticize me.	I'll never measure up.	Tight, tense, bad all over	Angry, she deserves what she gets	Tight jaw, body ready to explode	Yell at her, walk out of her house

When requirements are not fulfilled, your depressor becomes active, and you have unpleasant thoughts and body tension. The fixer then uses thoughts to try to repair or undo the negative mind-body state that the depressor created. These fixer thoughts, and the mental and physical pressure that comes with them, drive fixer behaviors, which then keep the depressor/fixer cycle going and lead to angry actions and outbursts.

2. You just experienced how your I-System works. It makes you angry and prevents you from accomplishing your goal. Let's do the map again, this time using your bridging awareness practices, and see what happens. Write the same goal in the oval. Before you start writing, listen to background sounds, feel your body's pressure on your seat, sense your feet on the floor, and feel the pen in your hand. Take your time. Once you're settled, keep feeling the pen in your hand, and start writing. Scatter your thoughts around the oval. Watch the ink go onto the paper, and listen to background sounds. Write for a couple of minutes.

WHAT I DON'T LIKE TO DO MOST MAP WITH BRIDGING

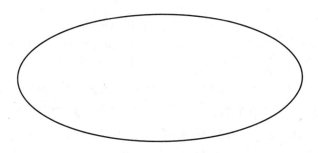

Look at the items on your map. The thoughts that come without excess body tension and mental pressure indicate executive functioning and the presence of your natural self. What are they?

_____

_____

_____

Both maps you just did had the same situation in the oval. In the first map, you saw how your I-System adds angry mind clutter, body tension, and depressor/fixer activity. In the second map, you quieted your I-System with your bridging awareness tools and shifted into executive functioning. In this state, your natural self in executive mode is in control. When your I-System is at rest, you can do things you don't like to do without getting angry or putting things off.

DEFUSING YOUR FIXER

Your day consists of one activity after another. Each activity you are doing or not doing throughout the day is either from executive functioning or driven by the fixer. Angry outbursts are only possible with an active fixer. The only time you can defuse and stop your fixer is in the midst of an activity. When you stop the depressor/fixer cycle and calm your I-System, your natural self controls the activity in executive mode. Throughout the day, notice the activity of your fixer: body tension, mental pressure, the depressor/fixer cycle, and storylines. When your fixer is active, use these steps to defuse it:

1. As soon as possible during an activity, notice any body tension, mental pressure, and spinning negative or angry storylines. They point you to your fixer.

2. Use bridging awareness practices and thought labeling to quiet your I-System.

3. Be on the lookout for new stories that the I-System's fixer (or embedded depressor) may spin about how the fixer can help you. These storylines impair your judgment and cause you to act in a way that makes you regret your actions afterward.

4. See the depressor that lies beneath the surface, and know that the fixer's real motive is to repair the powerless self (the fixer can't fix the powerless self, because the fixer keeps the I-System going).

5. Remember, it's not the activity you are doing, but who's doing it, that is important. Is it your I-System's powerless self, or is it your natural self, functioning in executive mode?

You know when you have defused your fixer, because your I-System is quiet, your body is calm, and your activities are being done by your natural self, not the pressure-driven fixer. You witness firsthand that the powerless self is a false belief caused by your active I-System. You are not broken and don't need fixing. Executive functioning is your birthright.

Mari, the harried mother mentioned earlier in this chapter, had trouble telling the difference between fixer thoughts and those from natural executive functioning, until she began using her bridging awareness practices throughout the day. Now she comes out of the shower with a relatively calm mind and body. When she looks at the clock, thinks *The kids will be late for school*, and feels her shoulders tighten, she knows that her usual response of yelling, "You'll be late for school! Hurry up!" comes from her fixer. She listens to the traffic sounds outside the window, feels her feet as she walks across the hall, feels her shoulders drop, and calmly gathers everyone. She has defused her fixer and returned to executive functioning.

In the heat of any situation, you, too, can convert the fixer into natural executive functioning. Remember, the only time to defuse and stop your fixer is *during* an activity. Use your fixer recognition tools for several days and then fill out the chart below.

Activity	Telltale Signs of Your Fixer	Anger Reduction Tools You Used	Results
Getting the kids ready for school	Breathing faster, shoulders pulled up, do-or-die sense of urgency	Listened to background sounds, stayed aware of my body	Calmly got kids ready for school
Thinking about my boss from hell	Chest pressure with storylines about how to deal with my boss	Recognized my fixer in action	Carried on with my day without being angry

We are so used to our fixer pushing us that we have come to accept what it does with an *It's just me* attitude. How many times have you ignored your body tension and dismissed your mind clutter, irritability, and anger with feelings of *It's just me*? Remember, when your I-System is on, you can defuse your fixer by simply being aware that it is active; then you use your bridging awareness tools to bring your awareness back to what you were doing. The tough part is telling the difference between the fixer and natural executive functioning. To do this, it helps to have a strong daily bridging awareness practice. Then as soon as you start to have body tension, storylines, mental pressure, and feelings of being pushed, you know it's the fixer. Once the physical and mental tension and the angry, "get-even" storylines have been released, this means that you have gone back to your natural self in executive mode.

YOU ARE NOT BROKEN AND DON'T NEED FIXING

1. Many people believe that their success in life is due to the drive and pressure of the fixer, and even say, "If it weren't for all this tension, I would never have accomplished anything." Do a map titled "What Will Happen to Me If I Give Up My Fixer." Jot down whatever comes to mind when you imagine giving up your fixer (for example, *I'll be taken advantage of, I'll lose my job, I'll never accomplish anything*, or *I won't be strong if I give up my anger*). Write for a couple of minutes. Describe your body tension at the bottom of the map.

WHAT WILL HAPPEN IF I GIVE UP MY FIXER MAP

WHAT WILL HAPPEN IF I GIVE UP MY FIXER?

Body Tension: _____

A. Look at your map and list some of your requirements:

_____

_____

_____

B. In this mind-body state, how do you act?

_____

Some people panic when they do this map. They feel as if they'll lose who they are and become weak if they give up their fixers. People think, *To give up my fixer would be like giving up my right arm!* and *If I let my fixer go, I'll go right down the tubes.* They fear that if they relax, they will be powerless and fail. This reliance on the fixer's power is the empty promise of the I-System that will never be fulfilled. The next map will demonstrate that when you quiet your I-System, you free yourself from the tyranny of your fixer and experience your limitless natural self.

2. Do the previous map again, this time using your bridging awareness practices. Before you start writing, listen to background sounds, feel your body's pressure on your seat, sense your feet on the floor, and feel the pen in your hand. Take your time. Once you're settled, keep feeling the pen in your hand, and start writing. Watch the ink go onto the paper, and listen to background sounds. Write for a couple of minutes.

> WHAT WILL HAPPEN IF I GIVE UP MY FIXER MAP WITH BRIDGING

WHAT WILL HAPPEN IF I GIVE UP MY FIXER?

A. List two fixer-driven behaviors that have caused difficulties in your life:

_____

_____

B. Are you ready to let go of them? Yes _____ No _____

C. When you are in executive-functioning mode instead of the spin of the I-System, do you feel that you are not broken and don't need fixing? Yes _____ No _____

With a quiet I-System, your natural self is in the driver's seat. In this unified mind-body state, you have access to your wellspring of healing, goodness, and wisdom, which gives you the strength and energy to take care of yourself and everything you have to do without angry and harmful outbursts.

WHO IS DOING IT?

"What should I do?" and "How should I handle my anger?" are frequently asked questions. But they aren't the right questions. The real issue is not *what* you should do or *how* you should do it, but *who* is doing it: your powerless self (active I-System) or natural self (executive mode). If your I-System is overactive and your powerless self is in charge, then nothing you do will ever be good enough, which gives rise to your angry outbursts. When your I-System is quiet, your natural self, functioning in executive mode, is in the driver's seat, calmly taking the best action to deal with any situation as it arises.

During the day, ask yourself *who* is doing the activity (walking, parenting, using the computer, paying bills, working, getting frustrated, playing, and so forth). Is it your anger-filled self, driven by an overactive I-System, or is it your natural self? Remember, it's not the activity, but who's doing it, that matters. The fixer can't *make* you powerful. Your self power is always present when your I-System is quiet and you are functioning in executive mode. Awareness of who's doing it helps you shift from the powerless self to the natural self that functions in executive mode. Try it and describe what happened:

_____

_____

_____

_____

_____

_____

DON'T LET YOUR FIXER FOOL YOU

The I-System is not a static system; it may try to fool you by creating more fixers. For your continued progress, it's important to recognize new fixers as they come up. Some examples are:

I'm doing better, so I can relax and not do as much bridging.

I'm good enough that I can do the maps in my head.

It's okay to explode once in a while if the situation warrants it.

I only need to bridge when I'm tense or angry.

If it feels good, I should do it, because it must be executive functioning.

Bridging means having free choice, so anytime I choose high-risk activities, it's okay.

Natural executive functioning is always effortless, so I don't need to practice anymore.

These fixers parade themselves as choices that come from natural executive functioning. But they have the same distinct signs you learned earlier in this chapter (body tension, mental pressure, urgent storylines, and not seeing the effects of your actions). What *is* new is that they offer themselves in a way that makes you feel good about them and you fail to notice the higher level of tension that is driving the choice. The fixer takes the path of least resistance. When you recognize the fixer and reduce your tension with your bridging awareness practices, your natural self makes the choice, free of the influence of the I-System.

PUTTING IT ALL TOGETHER

Remember, all your actions throughout the day are either from natural executive functioning or driven by the fixer. The fixer drives all angry outbursts. Recall that once a requirement (rule) is broken, the I-System is active. The depressor then grabs negative thoughts, which are spun into storylines that lead to an unpleasant mind-body state. Next the fixer jumps in to try to repair or undo this negative state. These fixer thoughts and a mind-body state that is filled with pressure are driving your fixer behavior. When you recognize your I-System at work and then use your anger reduction tools, your executive functioning is back in the driver's seat.

Ted was irritable most of the time. Even little things set him off. Prone to road rage, he often had to restrain himself from hurting others. For example, whenever someone drove too slowly, his neck bulged, his face reddened, and his head throbbed. Ted thought, *A guy driving twenty-five miles per hour in a forty-five zone should be shot!* He started using bridging awareness practices and thought labeling as effective tools to "cool down." Continuing his practices, he came to see that his multiple requirements—*The mail should be on time, I should not be put on hold, Others shouldn't speak disrespectfully about my team*—had frequently created meltdowns that caused him many problems. As he came to realize that his anger was an attempt to fix himself and the world, his disposition changed. In fact, one time, Ted and his wife were in the car rushing to deal with a family emergency, when they came upon a stopped car blocking an intersection. Ted's wife told him, "Get that guy moving." Ted got out of the car and, instead of getting angry, simply "saw an old guy who was lost, spent a few minutes calmly reassuring him by giving him directions, and then got back into the car." He then told us, "I had no idea I had that kindness in me."

Anger Reduction Tools

➤   Defuse the fixer.

➤   Recognize the depressor/fixer cycle.

➤   Convert fixer activity into executive functioning.

MBB RATING SCALE
BE STRONG WITHOUT ANGER

Date: _____

After using the tools in this chapter for a few days, check the box that best describes your practice: hardly ever, sometimes, usually, almost always.

How often do you...	Hardly Ever	Sometimes	Usually	Almost Always
Notice the fixer's never-ending pressure and tension?				
Become aware of the body sensations associated with the fixer?				
Realize that the fixer can never fix the powerless self?				
Find the depressor embedded in the fixer?				
Notice when the depressor/fixer cycle is active?				
Recognize the storylines that came with the fixer?				
Change your behavior by recognizing what happens as a result of your fixer-driven activities?				
Notice the difference between fixer-driven activities and those from natural executive functioning?				
Realize that the fixer is not necessary for your success?				
Notice the release of tension and excess pressure when you defuse your fixer in real time, using your anger reduction tools?				
Function better at home and at work?				

List the main body sensations you have when the fixer is in control:

_____

List angry or destructive behaviors that the fixer causes:

_____

List themes of storylines that come with fixer thoughts:

_____

_____

How did your behavior change when you noticed your fixer and shifted into executive mode?

_____

MBB QUALITY OF LIFE GAUGE

Date: _____

Only do this gauge when you have made a habit in your life of using the anger reduction tools from the first four chapters. It lets you measure your progress and keep track of your life-changing experiences.

Over the past seven days, how did you do in these areas?

Circle the number under your answer.	Not at all	Several days	More than half the days	Nearly every day
1. I've had positive interest and pleasure in my activities.	0	1	3	5
2. I've felt optimistic, excited, and hopeful.	0	1	3	5
3. I've slept well and woken up feeling refreshed.	0	1	3	5
4. I've had lots of energy.	0	1	3	5
5. I've been able to focus on tasks and use self-discipline.	0	1	3	5
6. I've stayed healthy, eaten well, exercised, and had fun.	0	1	3	5
7. I've felt good about my relationships with my family and friends.	0	1	3	5
8. I've been satisfied with my accomplishments at home, work, or school.	0	1	3	5
9. I've been comfortable with my financial situation.	0	1	3	5
10. I've felt good about the spiritual base of my life.	0	1	3	5
11. I've been satisfied with the direction of my life.	0	1	3	5
12. I've felt fulfilled, with a sense of well-being and peace of mind.	0	1	3	5

Score Key: Column Total   ____   ____   ____   ____

0-15 . . . . Poor

16-30 . . . . Fair   Total Score _____

31-45 . . . . .Good

46 and above .Excellent

CHAPTER 5

CONVERT ANGER INTO EXECUTIVE FUNCTIONING BY MANAGING REQUIREMENTS

Principles

Requirements that you do not defuse cause anger.

When you defuse requirements you stop angry outbursts and function in executive mode.

Mind-Body Language

Defusing requirements: When you use all your anger reduction tools, you handle a situation that used to make your I-System active with a ready and relaxed mind and body. Even when the picture of how you and the world should be is not fulfilled, the requirement is powerless to turn on your I-System.

YOUR OFF/ON ANGER SWITCH

The I-System, like a light switch, is either off or on. The natural state of the I-System is off. When it's off, you have a calm body and a clear mind, and you are in executive-functioning mode. The I-System is only turned on by requirements. When it's on, your body tenses and your mind spins with angry thoughts. You control the off/on switch by recognizing and defusing your requirements.

Figure 5.1 shows how your mind works. All thoughts naturally flow into the lower, executive-functioning loop when your I-System is switched off. In this unified mind-body state, you are in harmony and balance, and you live your best life. This lower loop is your birthright. No matter who you are or what you have been through, you can experience and express your natural self, right here, right now. Your natural self is always present. It doesn't depend on an idealized image or the ability to mimic good behavior. This lower loop isn't something to aim for; it's always with you, and you experience it automatically when your I-System is switched off. With your natural self in charge, you can work your way through any difficult situations that may come up. For example, when you are in the executive-functioning loop and you face a new tough situation, your natural self has the ability to deal with your constantly changing reality. Compare this to facing a new tough situation when you are in the I-System loop. Here, your coping and problem-solving skills are limited by requirements and the depressor/fixer cycle, resulting in stress overload and angry and harmful actions.

All thoughts begin as executive functioning and are free of the I-System. Requirements are formed when the I-System takes hold of thoughts to form a set of rules and a picture of how you and the world should be at any moment. As long as events do not break a requirement (rule), the I-System is off and all your thoughts, feelings, perceptions, and actions are from executive functioning. But when an event breaks a requirement, the I-System becomes active, with the depressor using negative thoughts to create unpleasant body tension. The fixer, in turn, uses thoughts to try to undo or repair the negative mind-body state the depressor caused. Because fixer thoughts come with mental and physical pressure, it drives fixer activities like angry outbursts and abuse. To keep the depressor/fixer cycle going, the I-System creates storylines.

In this chapter, you will map requirements that you have for yourself, others, and situations. Don't let your I-System fool you into thinking you can do maps in your head. When you put your thoughts on paper and notice your body sensations, a powerful mind-body free-association process takes place. The unexpected thought is often the requirement that lies beneath the surface. This is where your "aha" moments can happen. Each mapping exercise is placed in a way that increases your insights into each situation. The more you are in the executive-functioning loop, the quicker and easier it'll be to recognize and defuse your requirements as they arise in your life. Recognizing a requirement means that when you are distressed, you are able to identify the mental rule that has been broken about how you and the world should be. Defusing a requirement means that you are now able to face that same situation that used to cause distress and meltdowns with a ready, relaxed mind and body. No matter what the situation is, defusing requirements keeps your I-System turned off. Making a habit of using your anger reduction tools means you'll live more and more of your life in the anger-free executive-functioning loop.

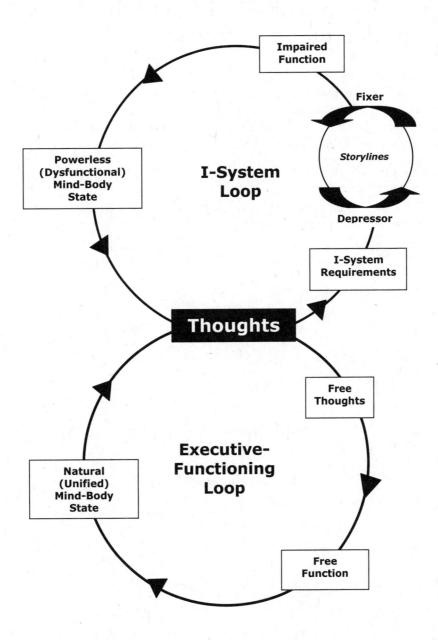

Figure 5.1 This is the I-System loop and the executive-functioning loop.

The mind works with thoughts. They flow in a natural way into the executive-functioning loop, where you take care of yourself and your responsibilities without angry outbursts. Free thoughts and free functioning are how you think, see the world, and act with an I-System at rest. When your thoughts become requirements for you and the world, you are pulled into the I-System loop, where the mind-body commotion of the I-System creates a life that is not satisfying and is filled with anger.

KEEP YOUR ANGER SWITCH OFF IN A DISTRESSING EXPERIENCE

1. There are times when someone's inappropriate behavior creates a stressful situation. Map the most distressing recent experience resulting from the behavior of another person. Write the behavior at the top of the map (*My boss lied to me*), and write how you wanted that person to act (*My boss shouldn't lie* or *My boss should tell the truth*) in the oval. Take a couple of minutes to write your thoughts around the oval as you think about that person's behavior.

DISTRESSING EXPERIENCE MAP

Other Person's Behavior: _____

A. What is your body tension, and how does it progress?

_____

_____

B. Is your distress and behavior due to the other person's behavior or the requirement you wrote in the oval?

_____

C. How do you act in this mind-body state?

_____

If you believe that your distress and behavior were a result of the other person's behavior, you are letting yourself be a victim of what has happened. As long as you do not see that how you wanted the other person to act is *your* requirement, you will suffer distress and stay in the I-System loop. When you recognize your requirement and see what it is doing to you, you start a dramatic mental and physical shift so that you are no longer a victim of other people's behavior.

2. Write the same behavior on the following line. In the oval again, write how you wanted that other person to act. Before you continue writing, listen to background sounds, feel your body's pressure on your seat, sense your feet on the floor, and feel the pen in your hand. Take your time. Once you feel settled, keep feeling the pen in your hand and start writing. Watch the ink go onto the paper and listen to background sounds. Write for a couple of minutes.

DISTRESSING EXPERIENCE MAP WITH BRIDGING

Other Person's Behavior: _____

A. How is this map the same as or different from the previous map?

_____

_____

B. How do you act in this mind-body state?

_____

C. Are you a victim of circumstance? Yes _____ No _____

D. Is the anger switch in your I-System turned off? Yes _____ No _____

On the first map in this exercise, the statement in the oval was a requirement, because it switched on your I-System. After you used your bridging awareness tools to quiet your I-System, that same statement was *no longer* a requirement. It became a natural thought or expectation, because your I-System was calm and your body tension and mind clutter were greatly reduced. You are now ready to deal with that same situation with a clear mind and relaxed body. Your mind-body bridging practice doesn't take away your natural expectations of how others should behave, but it does remove the distress that your requirements cause.

FINDING REQUIREMENTS THAT CAUSE YOUR DISTRESS

Tori was a high-powered, successful twenty-eight-year-old executive. She and her husband, Scott, agreed that he would be the stay-at-home parent, taking care of their children and the household responsibilities. This arrangement seemed to be working, but Tori was becoming more and more critical and irritated with Scott. She complained about dinner not being on the table when she came home, toys not being put away, and how Scott had forgotten to pick up her clothes at the cleaners. No matter how hard Scott tried, it seemed as if he always missed something. Tori said, "I almost didn't want to come home, because it made me feel angry and miserable." She learned about mind-body bridging and took to mapping like a fish to water.

Tori did a series of maps that totally changed her life. The first was a "Requirement for Scott" map. It was filled with "Scott should do" this and "Scott should do" that. The last map in the series was a "What Would It Look Like If Scott Fulfilled All My Requirements" map. After completing that map, she broke out sobbing and then couldn't stop herself from laughing. She had again written, "He should do" this and "He should do" that, but she finally wrote, "He would be my servant." Sobbing, she concluded, "I'm trying to make myself a dictator; I totally despise when men do that." Tori continued to integrate mind-body bridging practices into her everyday life and climb the corporate ladder. Soon she found coming home after work to be, in her words, "a true joy that I look forward to. Scott and I are closer than ever."

List the situations from the past few days that prompted you to become upset, tense, irritable, anxious, or overwhelmed. Realize that it's always the underlying requirement that you weren't yet aware of, not the event, that's causing your distress. Recognizing your underlying requirement prompts changes in your thoughts and actions.

Situation	How You Handled the Situation	Unfulfilled Requirement
My spouse said I'll never change.	I yelled, "Go to hell!" and didn't talk to him all day.	My spouse should accept me as I am.
I couldn't find my car keys.	I looked everywhere for them and became frustrated and angry.	I should always know where I put my car keys.

HANDLE YOUR NEMESIS WITH YOUR ANGER SWITCH OFF

1. Do a My Nemesis map. Pick the person who has been causing you the most grief, and write his or her name in the oval. Take a couple of minutes to jot whatever thoughts come to mind.

MY NEMESIS MAP

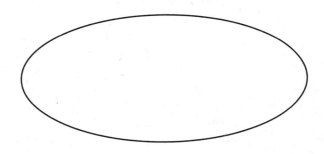

A. Describe your body tension and its progression:

_____

B. How do you act in this mind-body state?

_____

C. Identify the requirements on your map (for example, *She shouldn't bully me*):

_____

_____

_____

The commotion of your I-System has you feeling distressed, bitter, angry, and hopeless, and believing that anyone in your shoes would feel the same way. Now ask yourself, *Isn't it bad enough that the other person acts that way? Why do I have to let my I-System cause a meltdown, limiting my ability to deal with this person and the situation?* Remember, you have no control over others' behavior. You do have control over whether you defuse your requirements and reduce your anger in troubling relationships or tough situations.

2. Do this map using your bridging awareness practices. Write that same person's name in the oval. Before you continue writing, listen to any background sounds, feel your body's pressure on your seat, sense your feet on the floor, and feel the pen in your hand. Take your time. Once you feel settled, keep feeling the pen in your hand, and start writing. Watch the ink go onto the paper, and listen to any background sounds. For the next few minutes, jot down whatever thoughts pop into your mind.

MY NEMESIS MAP WITH BRIDGING

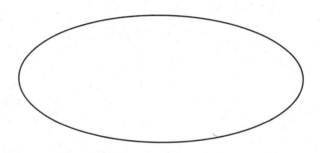

A. What is the difference in mind-body states between the two maps?

_____

_____

B. Can you see that it's your active I-System, not the nemesis, that's causing your distress?
   Yes _____ No _____

C. In real time, which anger reduction tools will you use to stay in executive mode while dealing with your nemesis?

_____

You now know for yourself that it's your active I-System, not the nemesis, that causes your anger and misery, keeping you from your natural self, which functions in executive mode. Also, this map shows the power of a strong daily bridging awareness practice. When you feel body tension, use your bridging awareness tools to create the emotional space you need to defuse requirements and deal with relationship problems and tough situations during your busy day.

LOOK BACK AT A VERY ANGER-FILLED DAY

Tom, a forty-three-year-old interstate truck driver, often spent a week at a time away from his family. Each time he came home, Tom would raise his voice and spend the evening telling everybody what they did wrong. On one anger-filled evening, he threw the dirty dishes into the trash as a lesson to the family to do the dishes right after dinner. After his wife threatened to leave him because of his angry outbursts, Tom joined a mind-body bridging anger management group, where he began learning mind-body bridging.

At first he was skeptical, but then he learned about his requirements. His Requirement map was very detailed (*Clean dishes, Clean laundry, Clean house, Lights turned off when leaving a room, Wife and children spending my money more wisely*). After recognizing his requirements, Tom said, "A light went on in my head. It's my requirements, not my family, that are causing my anger." Using his anger reduction tools, he began to defuse his requirements. Tom reported that his family remarked that he was much more pleasant to be around. He noticed that the more he used his anger reduction tools, the more his behavior changed. This naturally inspired his family to be more responsible.

1. Think about the most anger-filled day you've had in the last several weeks.

A. What were the demands on you that day?

_____

_____

B. How active was your depressor?

_____

_____

C. How did your fixer respond?

_____

_____

D. Did your storylines keep the depressor/fixer going? Yes _____ No _____

E. List the requirements you had for yourself and the situation:

_____

_____

F. How did you handle that day? Was your I-System or executive functioning in control?

_____

2. Now do a bridging map about that same anger-filled day. Before you start writing, listen to any background sounds, feel your body's pressure on your seat, sense your feet on the floor, and feel the pen in your hand. Take your time. Once you feel settled, keep feeling the pen in your hand, and start writing. Watch the ink go onto the paper, and listen to any background sounds. For the next few minutes, jot down whatever thoughts pop into your mind.

ANGER-FILLED DAY MAP WITH BRIDGING

ANGER-FILLED DAY

A. Is your mind cluttered or clear?

_____

B. Is your body tense or relaxed?

_____

C. How do you act in this mind-body state?

_____

D. Are you beginning to realize that your I-System, not the difficulties in your day, causes your distress? Yes _____ No _____

Your anger reduction tools will help you deal with any situation that comes up in your life.

MY PERFECT WORLD: POSSIBLE OR IMPOSSIBLE?

Do a How My World Would Look If My Requirements for Others Were Met map. Write your thoughts around the oval for a couple of minutes. Be as specific as you can (for example, *My spouse would always take care of me, Jason would not be a jerk, My neighbor would mind his own business, My coworkers would do their jobs*).

HOW MY WORLD WOULD LOOK IF MY REQUIREMENTS FOR OTHERS WERE MET MAP

HOW MY WORLD WOULD LOOK IF MY REQUIREMENTS FOR OTHERS WERE MET

Looking back over your map, what do you notice?

_____

_____

_____

_____

_____

_____

Even if your partner, boss, friend, or neighbor met all your requirements, your overactive I-System would always create new mental rules about how you and the world should be at any moment. Defusing requirements is a skill that helps you keep the I-System quiet and keeps your natural self in charge.

RECOGNIZE AND DEFUSE REQUIREMENTS TO GAIN CONTROL OF YOUR ANGER

When you get distressed, overwhelmed, and angry, that means you have a requirement that you aren't yet aware of. Use these steps to help you recognize and defuse your requirements:

1. Be aware of the first signs that your I-System is active (for example, notice specific body tension and depressor, fixer, and storyline activity). Let these signs prompt you to look for the requirement that lies beneath the surface.

2. Practice your skills by recognizing and defusing requirements in simple situations (for example, waiting for a long red light, having a dropped phone call, or dealing with rude clerks), and over time build to using your skills in more complex relationships and situations.

3. Use your thought labeling and bridging awareness practice tools to stop the commotion of the I-System and then find the requirement that lies beneath the surface. Remind yourself that it's *your* requirement about the activity, person, or situation—*not* the activity, person, or situation—that's causing your distress and anger.

4. Once you feel a release of body tension and mind clutter (whether over time or suddenly) about the situation, you have defused your requirement. The turmoil that used to be out of control melts into something that you can manage better.

Ronda, a single mom, learned that her twelve-year-old son was smoking. She became enraged, screamed and made threats, and ended up with a migraine. Later that week, when she found out he was smoking again, she began to feel her jaw tighten. Noticing that signal, Ronda realized that her I-System was switched on. She began listening to the sound of the dogs barking outside, which made her feel more settled and helped her to see her requirements: *My twelve-year-old son shouldn't smoke* and *I should be a better parent.* Ronda was now clear that it was her requirements, not his behavior, that caused her *added* distress. She was really disappointed in her son but didn't melt down. She was able to calm herself down enough to discuss the situation with her son, and they were able to choose a course of action.

Describe what happened when you used your anger reduction tools to defuse your requirements in a meltdown situation.

_____

_____

_____

_____

_____

When you quiet your I-System and defuse your requirements, you are in the executive-functioning loop (figure 5.1), where your natural self is in charge.

DIFFICULT-TO-DEFUSE REQUIREMENTS

Your I-System has been very busy defining how you and your world should be. Some requirements are easy to defuse, while others haven't budged. For the requirements that are harder for you to defuse, it helps to first focus on the behavior that triggered your requirement and then break that behavior down into smaller parts. For example, rather than deal with a general behavior like *My wife doesn't show me respect*, break it down into many smaller, specific behaviors: *The way she looks at me*, *The way she smiles at others*, *The critical tone of her voice*, *The sharp words she uses*. This lets you uncover very specific requirements: *She shouldn't give me that look*, *She should smile at me*, *She should speak in a loving voice*, and *She should use kind words*. Next, use your anger reduction tools on each of these requirements. Remember, after you recognize a requirement, it's ready to be defused in real time.

Over the next few days, recognize and defuse your requirements as they come up.

1. Describe which anger reduction tools worked best for you:

_____

_____

2. List the requirements that you were able to defuse and those that you were *not* able to defuse:

Was Able to Defuse	Could Not Defuse
My husband should let me know when he'll be late. *My son should pick up his towel.*	*My brother-in-law should get out of our lives.* *My son should do his homework.*

In dealing with a requirement like *My son should do his homework*, your I-System would have you believe that you are a bad parent because he doesn't do his homework. Remember, the goal of mind-body bridging is not to get your son to do his homework, but to defuse your requirement that he should do his homework. By doing so, you shift into executive mode and can use your natural wisdom to relate to your son in a different way. Figure 1.1 illustrates how your ability to do this expands.

3. From the previous chart, choose the requirement that has been the most difficult to defuse. Write it in the oval. Then, write your thoughts around the oval for a couple of minutes without editing them. Describe your body tension at the bottom of the map.

MOST DIFFICULT TO DEFUSE REQUIREMENT MAP

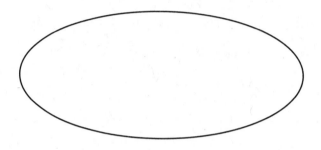

A. What is your body tension, and how does it progress?

_____

B. What are your depressors?

_____

C. What are your fixers?

_____

D. What are your storylines?

_____

E. What other requirements do you have?

_____

F. How do you act in this state?

_____

4. Do the map again, using your bridging awareness practices. Write the same requirement in the oval. Before you continue writing, listen to any background sounds, feel your body's pressure on your seat, sense your feet on the floor, and feel the pen in your hand. Take your time. Once you feel settled, keep feeling the pen in your hand, and start writing. Watch the ink go onto the paper, and listen to any background sounds. For the next few minutes, jot down whatever thoughts pop into your mind.

MOST DIFFICULT TO DEFUSE REQUIREMENT MAP WITH BRIDGING

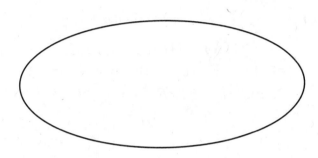

A. How is this map the same as or different from the previous map?

_____

_____

B. How would you act in the same situation with a quiet I-System?

_____

_____

Remember to use your anger reduction tools to defuse your requirements when the situation comes up again.

LET GO OF YOUR REQUIREMENTS

1. Do a What Will Happen If I Let Go of All My Requirements for the World? map. Write your thoughts around the oval for several minutes.

WHAT WILL HAPPEN IF I LET GO OF ALL MY REQUIREMENTS FOR THE WORLD? MAP

WHAT WILL HAPPEN
IF I LET GO OF ALL MY
REQUIREMENTS FOR THE
WORLD?

A. Does the commotion of your I-System leave you feeling weak and angry, and believing that you will lose control of your life? Yes _____ No_____

B. Write your level of body tension by each item on the map, using Ø for none, + for minimal, ++ for moderate, or +++ for severe. See the sample map that follows. Next, below, list those items that come with body tension, and identify their underlying requirements:

Item with Body Tension	Requirement

SAMPLE MAP: WHAT WILL HAPPEN IF I LET GO OF ALL MY REQUIREMENTS FOR THE WORLD?

No one will get anything done. +++

Nothing will be done right. +++

WHAT WILL HAPPEN IF I LET GO OF ALL MY REQUIREMENTS FOR THE WORLD?

People will take advantage of me. +++

My partner will see me as weak. +++

Things will go smoother. Ø

Len will spend too much time with his friends. ++

Item with Body Tension	Requirement
My partner will see me as weak.	My partner should see me as strong.
Len will spend too much time with his friends.	Len should spend less time with his friends.
People will take advantage of me.	People shouldn't take advantage of me.

2. Do the map again, this time using your bridging awareness practices. Before you start writing, listen to background sounds, feel your body's pressure on your seat, sense your feet on the floor, and feel the pen in your hand. Take your time. Once you're settled, keep feeling the pen in your hand, and start writing your thoughts. Watch the ink go onto the paper, and listen to background sounds. Write for a couple of minutes.

WHAT WILL HAPPEN IF I LET GO OF ALL MY REQUIREMENTS FOR THE WORLD? MAP WITH BRIDGING

WHAT WILL HAPPEN
IF I LET GO OF ALL MY
REQUIREMENTS FOR THE
WORLD?

What are the differences between the two maps?

_____

_____

_____

_____

Is it getting clearer that having I-System requirements is harmful to you and your world? Requirements limit your ability to deal well with other people and situations. When you quiet your I-System, your natural self can respond in an active, attentive, and healthy way in your relationships and situations. You'll be able to face each moment while having full access to your inner wellspring of healing, goodness, and wisdom. Your executive functioning self will take charge.

PUTTING IT ALL TOGETHER

Joe, a twice-divorced fifty-year-old father of two, was ordered by the court to take anger management classes after getting into an argument with his ex-wife that built up to his pushing her down and getting physical. He had nothing positive to say about his ex-wife (for example, he would go on about how it was all her fault and how he had been her victim). When he first heard about mind-body bridging, he was skeptical and wasn't sure if it would do him any good. Joe decided that he would give it his best shot. When he returned for session two, he reported that he was becoming aware of his active I-System (spinning angry thoughts, jaw tensing, fist tightening) just before being flooded with feelings of rage. This recognition, along with his thought labeling and bridging awareness tools, helped Joe gain a sense of self-control. The intensity of his angry and out-of-control emotions began to decrease as he started mapping. He learned about how his requirements made his I-System active. When he did a How the World Should Be map, Joe was surprised at how many requirements he had that were related to his feelings of anger toward his ex-wife; for example, *She should pay more attention to me*, *She should do what I want*, and *She shouldn't blame me and get on my case*, to mention just a few. As he continued to recognize and defuse his I-System requirements, Joe reported that he could now manage his feelings of anger toward his ex-wife and that these feelings no longer had the intensity that they once had. As he learned to switch off his I-System by using all of his anger reduction tools, his natural self thrived. Joe no longer saw himself as a victim, and his angry outbursts stopped.

Defusing requirements is a vital anger reduction tool. Remember, using all of your anger reduction tools allows you to become good at switching off your I-System. Turning off your anger switch gives you access to your natural self, which functions in executive mode.

Anger Reduction Tool

➢ Defuse your requirements for others and for situations.

MBB RATING SCALE
CONVERT ANGER INTO EXECUTIVE FUNCTIONING BY MANAGING REQUIREMENTS

Date: _____

After using the tools in this chapter for a few days, check the box that best describes your practice: hardly ever, sometimes, usually, almost always.

How often do you...	Hardly Ever	Sometimes	Usually	Almost Always
Recognize that requirements always trigger your I-System and limit your natural self?				
Recognize that requirements are responsible for your anger?				
Prevent anger by defusing a requirement?				
See that the requirements you have for others or situations trap you, keeping you from being your natural self?				
Cut off storylines by using thought labeling and bridging awareness practices?				
Notice the powerless self when it is in charge?				
Experience the powerless self as a myth of the I-System?				
Experience your natural self, functioning in executive mode, when your I-System is switched off?				
Know it's your natural self when you are naturally functioning moment by moment (executive-functioning loop)?				
Come to appreciate aspects of your everyday life?				
Experience that you are connected to a wellspring of healing, goodness, and wisdom?				
Find that your relationships have improved?				
Function better at home and at work?				

List three requirements you defused that previously caused a meltdown. How did you deal with the situation in the executive-functioning loop?

_____

_____

_____

CHAPTER 6

BUILD AN ANGER-FREE FOUNDATION FOR YOUR RELATIONSHIPS

Principles

An active I-System affects your relationships in a negative way.

When your I-System is at rest, you have the power to build an anger-free foundation for your relationships.

RELATIONSHIPS AND YOUR I-SYSTEM

The requirements of your I-System get you into relationships you shouldn't be in, keep you out of those that are good for you, and, most importantly, create chaos in your present relationships.

Ari had an issue with jealousy. He would get angry if he thought his girlfriend might be flirting with another man. If another man spoke to her in public, Ari quickly started arguing and making threats. After his girlfriend left him, Ari took a mind-body bridging class at the urging of a coworker. Using his anger reduction tools, Ari did a few two-part maps. He began to see that his low self-esteem and insecurity made his I-System active, which led to violent and harmful actions. When he dug deeper into his relationship maps, it became clear to him that his being jealous and exploding in anger were related to, as he put it, "the blinder my I-System put on me that kept me from seeing the whole picture." He had never realized that it was his low self-esteem, not his girlfriend's actions, that was behind his angry outbursts. Before, whenever he thought about whether his girlfriend was faithful, or even what another man intended toward her, his I-System would always consume him. He had never been able to take a complete look at the situations, because "it was impossible with a revved-up I-System."

As he progressed in group, healthier behaviors and approaches became clear to him, and his self-confidence improved. In fact, he decided, for the first time since he was a teen, that he did not need a girlfriend to build his self-worth. Ari kept using his anger reduction tools in all parts of his life, and his self-esteem increased as he lived more and more in executive mode.

It's vital to remember that defusing requirements like *He shouldn't be so demanding*, *My wife shouldn't speak to other men*, and *No one should show interest in my partner* doesn't mean giving up your natural expectation that you and your partner behave in an acceptable way. What it does mean is that when your partner acts in a way that used to rile you up because of your requirement, your natural self will now respond to the situation in an appropriate way, without losing control of your anger. If that requirement were not defused, your ability to respond would be limited by your active I-System.

The requirements you have for yourself constantly create inner distress, interfere with your relationships, impair your quality of life, and keep you from being who you are meant to be. You know how painful it is when others don't accept who you are. But what about the pain you put yourself through when you don't accept yourself? Can you imagine the relief you feel when your inner critic is quiet, letting your natural self be in the driver's seat? When you defuse the relentless self-demands (requirements for yourself), you strengthen the foundations of your relationships. The real stressor in your relationships is not the other person or who you are, but your active I-System. Once it has been made active by a requirement, your depressor pulls the rug out from under your self-esteem, making you feel small, weak, vulnerable, and inadequate. Your fixer jumps in with angry, controlling behavior to counter the way the depressor makes you feel. When your I-System is quiet, you clearly see that your negative thoughts are just thoughts, your body is calm, and you know the truth: you are whole and complete, not weak and damaged. This is the anger-free base for your relationships.

KEEP THE PAST IN THE PAST

Is your past restricting how you live your life, preventing you from being who you are meant to be right here, right now? Past experiences can either positively or negatively affect your life.

1. Do a How I Got to Be the Way I Am map. Around the oval, write how you got to be the way you are. Write for a couple of minutes. A sample map follows.

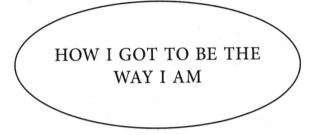

HOW I GOT TO BE THE WAY I AM MAP

A. What is your body tension, and how does it progress?

_____

B. What storyline themes run through your map?

_____

_____

C. Describe when and how often you use these storylines, for example, when you feel like a success or failure, when you're sad or happy, or when you're bored or busy:

_____

D. How do you act when the above storylines are active?

_____

The I-System uses stories (positive and negative, about the past and future) to keep you from living in the present. No matter what they are about, storylines tense your body, limit your awareness, and pull you away from being able to function in the present moment. In doing so, they strengthen your false belief in the powerless self. Being more aware of your storylines quiets your I-System and puts you in the executive-functioning loop, where thoughts of the past are simply thoughts, without the heat and spin of the I-System.

SAMPLE MAP: HOW I GOT TO BE THE WAY I AM

Poor school district.

Mom was depressed.

HOW I GOT TO BE THE WAY I AM

Dad wasn't around much.

I always knew Mom loved me, but she didn't show it.

One of my teachers helped me feel good about myself.

I was physically abused.

I was fine before my parents divorced.

My friends always had my back.

I never gave up.

I grew up in foster care.

A. What is your body tension, and how does it progress? *Jaw tight, and then I start grinding my teeth.*

2. Do another How I Got to Be the Way I Am map, this time using your bridging awareness practices. Before writing, listen to any background sounds, feel your body's pressure on your seat, sense your feet on the floor, and feel the pen in your hand. After you feel settled, jot around the oval whatever thoughts pop into your mind. Keep listening to background sounds and feeling the pen in your hand. Watch the ink go onto the paper. Write for a couple of minutes.

HOW I GOT TO BE THE WAY I AM MAP WITH BRIDGING

(oval) HOW I GOT TO BE THE WAY I AM

A. How is this map different from your first How I Got to Be the Way I Am map?

_____

_____

_____

B. What insights have you gained from doing this bridging map?

_____

_____

_____

_____

When you continue to do maps like the one above, your past remains the past.

BE YOURSELF RIGHT HERE AND NOW

"Being in the moment" has become a popular theme for improving yourself and your relationships. But the problem is not being in the moment, because there has never been a human being who wasn't in the moment. You can only breathe now; you can only act now; your heart can't pump yesterday's blood or tomorrow's blood. It can only beat right here, right now. It's impossible to not live in the present moment. The problem is that the I-System, when activated by requirements, uproots you from experiencing and expressing the essence of who you are right here, right now. Let's see how it works.

Do a How I Want to Be Right Here, Right Now map. *Inside* the circle, write how you would like to be right here, right now (for example, *organized, strong, calm, attractive*). Be specific! After you have listed at least six qualities, write the opposite of each quality *outside* the circle. Connect the quality inside the circle with a line to its opposite, outside the circle. If needed, see the sample map that follows.

HOW I WANT TO BE RIGHT HERE, RIGHT NOW MAP

SAMPLE MAP: HOW I WANT TO BE RIGHT HERE, RIGHT NOW

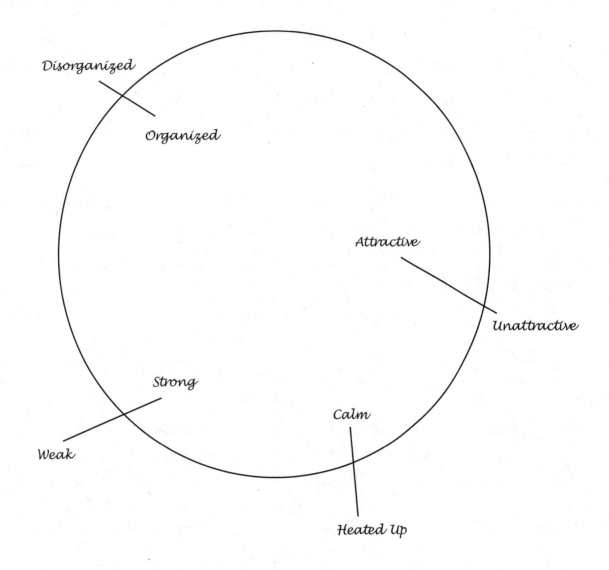

1. How do the qualities *inside* the circle make you feel?

_____

_____

_____

2. How do the qualities *outside* the circle make you feel?

_____

_____

_____

If the qualities *outside* the circle create body tension and negative emotions, they are triggers. Remember, a trigger (an event or thought) is a sign that a requirement has made your I-System active. This means that those opposite qualities (about how you want to be) *inside* the circle are requirements. Once your requirement is defused, the trigger no longer turns on your I-System.

3. From your map, list your triggers and requirements about how you want to be:

Trigger	Requirement
Being disorganized	*I should be organized.*

When your I-System takes hold of your natural expectation, that expectation turns into a requirement (an ideal picture of who you are). This leads to mind clutter and body tension. Your self-esteem suffers, and whatever you do will never be good enough. This can lead you to act from anger and abuse others.

MIRROR, MIRROR ON THE WALL

How's your self-image? Do you really want to know? Are you ready to let it all hang out?

1. Let's do a Mirror map. Find a quiet place and look in a mirror. Before you start writing, really look at yourself for a minute or so. Next, write around the oval any thoughts and feelings that come to mind about what you see. Try not to censor anything. Glance back at the mirror several times and keep writing whatever comes to mind. Describe your body tension at the bottom of the map.

MIRROR MAP

```
          _____
        /                      \
       /                        \
      |         MIRROR           |
       \                        /
        _____/
```

Body Tension: _____

A. Is your I-System active? Yes _____ No _____

B. What are your storylines?

_____

_____

C. Is your depressor causing you to experience your face as an enemy and making you feel unacceptable?
   Yes _____ No _____

D. What are your requirements?

_____

_____

E. How do you act when you don't accept yourself?

_____

2. Do another Mirror map, this time using your bridging awareness practices. Before writing, listen to any background sounds, feel your body's pressure on your seat, sense your feet on the floor, and feel the pen in your hand. Now look in the mirror and keep listening to background sounds. Take your time. After you feel settled, jot around the oval whatever thoughts pop into your mind. Keep listening to background sounds and feeling the pen in your hand. Watch the ink go onto the paper. Write for a couple of minutes.

MIRROR MAP WITH BRIDGING

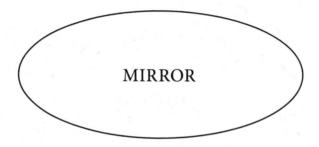

A. How is this map different from your first Mirror map?

_____

_____

B. Did the facial features you see in the mirror change? Yes _____ No _____

C. Do you now have a new level of self-acceptance? Yes _____ No _____

D. How do you act when you accept yourself?

_____

Take a good look at your image in the mirror every morning and again at night. Let your thoughts flow freely, and notice your body tension. See the telltale signs of your active I-System. Be aware of your depressor, your fixer, and, most important, your requirements for yourself. When you use your bridging awareness practices, the foundation of who you are becomes stable and your emotions will balance themselves. Over time observe how your self-image improves without your having to try to fix yourself. This shift in self-acceptance that comes with continued use of your anger reduction tools shows that you are capable of having anger-free relationships.

ANGER REDUCTION TOOLS TO IMPROVE YOUR SELF-IMAGE

- *Thought labeling:* When a negative thought pops into your mind, remember, a thought is just a thought. Label your negative thoughts as mere thoughts, and return to what you were doing. For example, when *I'll never control my anger* pops into your mind, say to yourself, *I'm having the thought, "I'll never control my anger," and it's just a thought.*

- *Bridging awareness practices:* When you notice negative self-talk and body tension in your life, know that it as a sign that your I-System is switched on, tune in to your senses, and then go back to what you were doing.

- *Storyline awareness:* When you catch yourself going over stories about negative things that have happened to you, notice the repeating themes, recognize them as storylines, and return to the task at hand. It doesn't matter if the stories are true or false, positive or negative. Remember, it's not your negative thoughts that get you down or your positive thoughts that pull you up; your storylines create mind clutter and fill every cell of your body with tension, keeping the depressor/fixer dance going. When your I-System gets hold of your stories, that's what takes you away from the present.

- *Mapping:* Use the two-part mind-body maps. The first map helps you find your requirements that reinforce your negative self-beliefs. Noticing your body tension is what helps you find these requirements. Use your bridging awareness practices on the second map to see the truth about negative self-beliefs and return to executive functioning.

- *Defusing requirements:* When you notice body tension and negative self-talk, quiet your I-System, and then find your requirement (for example, if the negative self-talk is *I'm power-less*, the requirement is *I should be powerful*. Remember, the distress you feel now is from an I-System that's active, not the situation or your negative thoughts. Once you feel a release of body tension and mind clutter (whether over time or suddenly) about the situation, you have defused your requirement. Your natural self that functions in executive mode is back in the driver's seat.

POWERING YOUR SELF-IMAGE

Use your anger reduction tools today to keep your negative self-image and self-talk from getting you down, making you angry, and getting in the way of your life. Then fill out the chart below.

Negative Self-Image	Body Tension	What Anger Reduction Tools Did You Use and How?	Body Sensations	How Your Behavior Changed After Using Your Tools
I'm not smart enough to get ahead in the world.	Chest tight, shallow breath	Labeled my thoughts. Listened to hum of air conditioner.	Chest and breathing relaxed	Wasn't as depressed. Accomplished a lot on the job today.
I'm unlovable.	Gut cramps	I immediately recognized the thought "I should be lovable" as a requirement.	Calmer	"Light came on," day went smoothly, and I wasn't defensive or angry.

Your I-System requirements about how you "should be" are getting in the way of your self-image. These requirements keep you from believing and trusting in who you are, right here and now. Recall that you will never be smart enough, attractive enough, or calm enough to satisfy a requirement. When the requirement isn't satisfied, your I-System heats up with negative thoughts and body tensions. No matter who you are or what you have been through, your mind-body anger reduction tools can strengthen your self-image and change your life.

REQUIREMENTS FOR YOURSELF

1. List three situations from the last several days where your requirements for yourself activated your I-System. For example, *I should know the answer when my boss asks me a question, I should be home on time, I shouldn't be alone, I shouldn't make a mistake.*

Situation	Requirement for Yourself
At our morning meeting, my boss asked me a question.	*I should know the answer when my boss asks me a question.*

2. Fill out this chart based on what you listed in the chart above:

Body Tension and Its Progression When Your Requirement Is Met	Body Tension and Its Progression When Your Requirement Is *Not* Met
Stomach tight, foot jiggles, hands grip chair arms tightly	*Face hot, dry mouth, pressure builds in my chest*

3. Fill out the next chart for each requirement from the previous one:

Storylines When Meeting Requirement	Storylines When Not Meeting Requirement
I am so good, It's a relief, It's over, I know how to deal with him.	*I'll never have all the answers, My boss is wrong, He's not a good boss, I'm pissed, It's always the same.*

4. Fill out the next chart using the same requirements:

Your Behavior When Meeting Requirement	Your Behavior When Not Meeting Requirement
Puffed up and laughed too loud, interrupted my colleagues	*Angry and irritable all day*

The I-System has you between a rock and a hard place. When your requirements for yourself aren't met, your depressor moves into the driver's seat, leaving you powerless. Even when you are able to meet your requirements, the fixer moves into the driver's seat, and enough is never enough. It's not a matter of meeting or not meeting your requirements, but one of defusing them. When your requirements are defused, your natural self, in executive mode, is in the driver's seat, and you naturally take the right action moment by moment.

5. Using your bridging awareness practices, listen to background sounds, feel your body's pressure on your seat, sense your feet on the floor, and feel the pen in your hand. When you're settled, label your thoughts and go over each requirement you listed in the first chart in this exercise. What have you noticed about each of your requirements after mind-body bridging?

Requirement One:

_____

_____

_____

Requirement Two:

_____

_____

_____

Requirement Three:

_____

_____

_____

YOUR EVERYDAY RELATIONSHIPS

Now that you know how critical it is for your self-esteem and well-being that you have a quiet I-System, it's time to tackle your relationships. We all have natural hopes and desires for ourselves and others (respectful, dependable, supportive, honest, helpful, and so forth). Each of us uses these natural expectations to guide us as we interact with others. When the I-System takes hold of these expectations and makes them requirements, they harm our relationships, close off our natural executive functioning, and limit our ability to relate to others.

Let's look at what happens when your natural expectations for yourself are turned into requirements and how they harm your relationships and lower your self-esteem. This exercise is about the requirements you have for yourself in your relationships with coworkers, in-laws, neighbors, grocery clerks, and so on (for example, *I shouldn't be so angry with my father-in-law, I should be more assertive with my coworkers, I should be more caring*).

Answer the following questions:

1. My relationship with _____

A. What natural expectations do you have for yourself in this relationship? Example: I should set better boundaries with my neighbor.

_____

_____

B. How do you feel and act, and what is your body tension when you don't follow through? Example: I get angry with myself and my neighbor, I get a headache.

_____

C. What are your requirements about this relationship?

_____

_____

D. Use your anger reduction tools to defuse your requirements and change this relationship.

2. List your natural expectations for yourself in other everyday relationships; be as specific as possible. Note if they have been made into requirements.

Natural Expectation	Body Tension If Expectation Is Not Met	Is It Now a Requirement?
I want to get along with my coworker.	*Knot in stomach, shoulders tight*	*Yes*
Being on time to meet a friend	*None*	*No*

When your requirement isn't met, you are in distress, with your I-System creating mind clutter and body tension. Recognize your requirements and use your anger reduction tools to defuse them. When your natural expectation isn't met, you feel let down, but you are able to handle the situation without angry outbursts.

YOUR MOST IMPORTANT RELATIONSHIP

1. Map your expectations for yourself in your most important relationship. Write the person's name in the oval. Around the oval, write your thoughts about how you should be in that relationship (for example, *I shouldn't criticize Jay, I shouldn't upset him when he's tired, I should make him happy*). There's no right or wrong. Be specific and work quickly for the next few minutes.

HOW I SHOULD BE IN MY MOST IMPORTANT RELATIONSHIP MAP

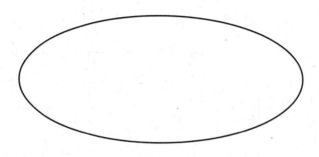

Look at each item and notice any body tension you have when you think about meeting that expectation for how you should be in that relationship. Look again at each item and notice your body tension when you think about *not* meeting that expectation. Thoughts that come with body tension are your requirements.

For each item with body tension, describe how you act when you don't meet that requirement:

_____

_____

_____

_____

2. Do the map again, writing the person's name in the oval. Before you continue writing, listen to background sounds, feel your body's pressure on your seat, sense your feet on the floor, and feel the pen in your hand. Take your time. Once you're settled, keep feeling the pen in your hand, and start writing any thoughts that come to mind about that relationship. As you write, keep paying attention to background sounds, feeling the pen in your hand, and watching the ink go onto the paper. Write for a couple of minutes.

HOW I SHOULD BE IN MY MOST IMPORTANT RELATIONSHIP MAP WITH BRIDGING

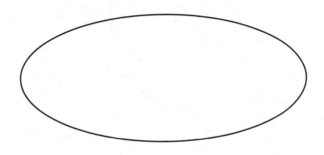

A. In this mind-body state, how do you act?

_____

_____

B. How can this map help you in your relationship?

_____

_____

The release of body tension means you have moved from the I-System loop into the executive-functioning loop (see figure 5.1), where you can now act in a natural way. You still have thoughts or natural expectations about how you should be in your relationship, but this release of body tension frees you to act in a different way.

When your active I-System switches off, you let go of your requirements and create new ways to relate in your most important relationships, free of anger.

TRANSFORM YOUR MOST IMPORTANT RELATIONSHIP

You have been building a foundation for your relationship by defusing your requirements for yourself. Now it's time to focus on the requirements you have for the person who is most important to you.

1. Do a map of how you think the person most important to you should act. Write that person's name in the oval. Around the oval, write your thoughts for how you want that person to act. Write for a couple of minutes.

```
┌─────────────────────────────────────────────────────┐
│      HOW THE PERSON MOST IMPORTANT TO ME             │
│              SHOULD ACT MAP                           │
└─────────────────────────────────────────────────────┘
```

                    HOW
            _____
                SHOULD ACT

Look back over the items on the map and label your requirements with an "R." Next, under each requirement, write what storylines ("SL") you have when the other person does not meet that requirement. Below each thought, note whatever body tension ("BT") you have when the other person doesn't meet your requirement. Take your time while doing this map. See the sample map that follows.

SAMPLE MAP: HOW THE PERSON MOST IMPORTANT TO ME SHOULD ACT

(R) *He needs to do more around the house.*
(SL) *I do all the work, and I feel angry and taken for granted.*
(BT) *Tight chest*

(R) *She should appreciate me.*
(SL) *Why doesn't she appreciate me?*
(BT) *Stomachache*

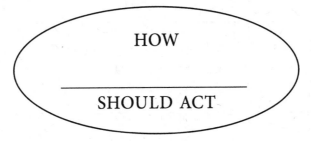

(R) *He should take me out to eat more often.*
(SL) *I feel frustrated and ignored.*
(BT) *Headache*

(R) *He should compliment me more.*
(SL) *I feel ignored; he doesn't care.*
(BT) *Tight chest*

(R) *She should respect how hard I work.*
(SL) *I don't get any slack; I should be able to relax.*
(BT) *Shoulders tight*

(R) *She should pay attention to me.*
(SL) *I feel angry and unimportant.*
(BT) *Sinking feeling in stomach*

R = Requirement

SL = Storyline when requirement is unfulfilled

BT = Body tension when requirement is unfulfilled

A. For each item on your map, fill out the following chart:

Requirement	How Do You Act When the Most Important Person to You Doesn't Meet Your Requirement?	How Does It Affect Your Relationship?
She should appreciate me.	Get angry, don't talk to her	Creates distance and tension

B. Now, using your bridging awareness practices and thought labeling, when you feel settled, go back over your relationship requirements from the chart above and fill out the chart below.

Requirement	How Do You Act When the Most Important Person to You Doesn't Meet Your Requirement?	How Does It Affect Your Relationship?
She should appreciate me.	Disappointed, but can talk to her	Makes us closer

When there is a release of body tension, it shows that you are ready to defuse your requirement when the situation comes up again.

2. Write the name of the person from the previous map in the oval below. Next, choose the requirement that still causes you the *most distress* when it's not met (for example, *She should appreciate me*), and write that on the line below. Now write your thoughts around the oval for a couple of minutes, describing how things would look if that person *did* meet that requirement. Use as much detail as possible. For example, if the requirement is *She should appreciate me*, you might write, *She would not be critical*, *She would always have dinner ready*, *She would say yes more*, or *She would be nice to my brother*.

HOW THINGS WOULD LOOK IF MY REQUIREMENT WERE MET MAP

Requirement that causes me the most distress: _____

HOW THINGS WOULD LOOK IF _____ MET MY REQUIREMENT

A. Do you really think this will happen? Yes _____ No _____

B. Do you recognize that an active I-System will keep creating requirements for you and your relationship? Yes _____ No _____

Many people smile when they do this map, because they see clearly how the I-System works. They see that when they defuse their requirements, they can handle personal boundaries and basic rights from a place of strength and without angry and harmful actions.

WHO STILL BUGS YOU?

Mind-body bridging is not about finding out how you should relate to others; it *is* about finding out how the I-System restricts you and your relationships.

1. Do a requirement map for someone who is still bugging you. In the oval, write the name of the person who continues to trouble you the most. Around the oval, write your expectations for how that person should act. Write for a couple of minutes.

TROUBLING PERSON MAP

MY EXPECTATIONS FOR

_____

A. Next, under each item, list any body tension you have when the other person does *not* meet that expectation. Those items are requirements.

B. Describe how the fixer and depressor are dancing in this relationship:

_____

_____

C. What are your storylines?

_____

_____

D. In this mind-body state, how do you act?

_____

2. Do the map again, this time using your bridging awareness practices. Write the same person's name in the oval. Before you continue writing, listen to background sounds, feel your body's pressure on your seat, sense your feet on the floor, and feel the pen in your hand. Take your time. Once you're settled, keep feeling the pen in your hand and start writing any thoughts that come to mind about how that person should act. Watch the ink go onto the paper and keep listening to background sounds. Write for a couple of minutes.

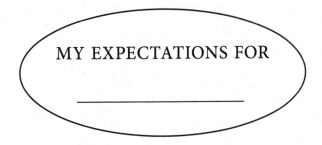

TROUBLING PERSON MAP WITH BRIDGING

MY EXPECTATIONS FOR

_____

A. How is this map different from the previous map?

_____

B. What body sensations do you have when you imagine that person not doing what you wrote down on this map? The absence of body tension means that the item is not a requirement and that it is a natural expectation.

_____

C. In this mind-body state, how do you act?

_____

D. When your I-System is switched off, your natural goals and expectations do not become pressure-driven requirements. Go back to the previous map and use your anger reduction tools on any remaining requirements you had for that person.

When you recognize and defuse your requirements for both yourself and others, your natural self, with its whole range of experiences, emotions, and gifts, enters into each and every relationship. There is no cookbook for keeping relationships free of anger, only the golden key: an I-System at rest.

PUTTING IT ALL TOGETHER

When you defuse requirements for yourself, you are released from the grip of an active I-System, and you have the power to build an anger-free foundation for your relationships. You now have access to your natural self in executive mode, which acts in a healthy and appropriate way.

Tools to Defuse Requirements for Yourself

1. Be aware of the first signs that your I-System has been switched on (body tension, self-critical or angry thoughts, or storylines). This will prompt you to look for the hidden requirement.

2. Use your thought labeling and bridging awareness practice tools to stop the uproar of the I-System.

3. Recognize that it's *your* requirement for yourself, not the other person or the situation, that's causing your distress and anger.

4. Use your anger reduction tools to find and defuse your requirement.

5. You'll know you have defused the requirement when you feel a release of body tension and self-critical mind clutter. When the situation comes up again, your natural self is in the driver's seat, and you are able to deal with it in a calm and appropriate way.

As you defuse your requirements for yourself, you create the power to improve your relationships. When you defuse both sets of your requirements (for how you and the other person should be), your natural self, in executive mode, will naturally build relationships that are healthy and free of anger.

Anger Reduction Tools

➢ Defuse your requirements for yourself.

➢ Defuse your requirements for your relationships.

MBB RATING SCALE
BUILD AN ANGER-FREE FOUNDATION FOR YOUR RELATIONSHIPS

Date: _____

After using the tools in this chapter for a few days, check the box that best describes your practice: hardly ever, sometimes, usually, almost always.

How often do you...	Hardly Ever	Sometimes	Usually	Almost Always
Notice that requirements always switch on your I-System, causing problems in your relationships?				
Notice that requirements keep your negative self-image going?				
Improve relationships by defusing requirements?				
See that your requirements for yourself trap you and keep you from being who you really are?				
Experience yourself as far more than who you thought you were?				
Notice that all you need to do to act from executive functioning is quiet your I-System?				
Notice when your powerless self is in the driver's seat?				
Experience your powerless self as a myth of the I-System?				
Recognize when you are in executive-functioning mode?				
Appreciate your natural self (who you are when you function naturally moment by moment)?				
See everyday life in a new light?				
Notice yourself connected to your wellspring of healing, goodness, and wisdom?				
Notice that your relationships have improved?				
Act better at home and at work?				
Notice an increase in your self-esteem?				

List three requirements for yourself in your relationship that used to make you angry and that you now deal with by being in executive mode:

_____

_____

_____

CHAPTER 7

STOP ANGER FROM INTERFERING WITH YOUR HEALTH AND WELL-BEING

Principles

Your undefused requirements restrict who you are and your ability to take care of yourself.

Defusing requirements leads to wellness and a balanced life.

Mind-Body Language

Mind-body bridging (MBB) action steps: Actions you take to achieve a goal that come from the two-part mind-body mapping process and are carried out by your natural self in executive mode.

WHO'S IN CHARGE OF YOUR SELF-CARE?

You know that unmanaged anger, no matter where it's directed, not only affects how you get along in the world, but also has a profound impact on your health and well-being. It's common knowledge that peptic ulcer disease, headaches, high blood pressure, strokes, heart attacks, and many other medical conditions are related to anger that was poorly managed.

By now you know the truth about your I-System. When your active I-System is in charge of your emotions, it limits your lifestyle and healthy choices. Your unmanaged stress and anger reduces your quality of life and increases your chances of having illness, accidents, and even an early death.

Larry, a hard-driving twenty-eight-year-old businessman, spent most of his time competing in business and sports. He denied that his headaches and rare bouts of dizziness were anything to worry about. His high blood pressure was only found during a life insurance physical. He was angry that his life insurance premium was much higher than his agent had thought it would be. He stopped his insurance and didn't seek medical treatment. It was only after taking part in an MBB executive training program that he came to see that when his requirements were broken (*Company X should have purchased my services, My employees should not make mistakes, I should not have medical problems*), he would get angry right away, blame others, and then direct his focus on another challenge. When he mapped his business issues, he came to see that his fixer was not only hiding his depressor (*I'm weak, out of control, fragile*), but also keeping him from seeing the results of his actions. Toward the end of his MBB executive training program, he not only began to make better business choices, but also sought medical treatment and started to take better care of himself.

This chapter gives you the chance to put your natural self in charge of your health and wellness as you uncover even more requirements. Also, you will learn a powerful new tool called *MBB (mind-body bridging) action steps*. You use the two-part mapping process to find actions you may take to reach a goal that are free of the influence of your I-System. When your I-System is at rest, you are in executive mode, where you naturally achieve wellness, and take care of yourself and your tasks without anger affecting your choices.

Gene, a healthy, upbeat executive, was diagnosed with prostate cancer at age fifty. His outlook on life changed, and he became irritable, disagreed sharply with associates, and was more critical with his family. Despite the urging of his doctor, Gene put off getting medical treatment. His doctor finally referred him to mind-body bridging. When he did maps about his prostate cancer, he saw his many requirements and how his I-System used his thoughts about cancer to control his life. Gene saw how his fixer kept him from admitting the reality of his cancer and caused him to get angry with those around him: "It was my I-System that made me a victim, not my cancer." Gene's MBB action steps included working closely with his medical team to choose the right course of action. Gene stated, "I'm now a survivor rather than a victim."

WHO DO YOU THINK YOU ARE?

Do a Who Am I? map. Inside the circle, write the qualities that best describe who you are. After you have listed at least six qualities, outside the circle write the opposite of each quality, and connect it with a line. If needed, see the sample map that follows.

WHO AM I? MAP

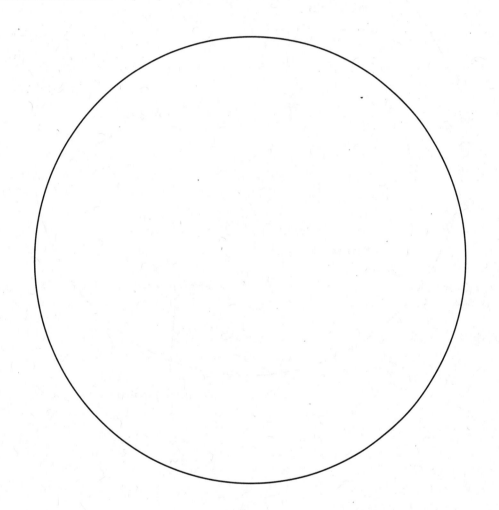

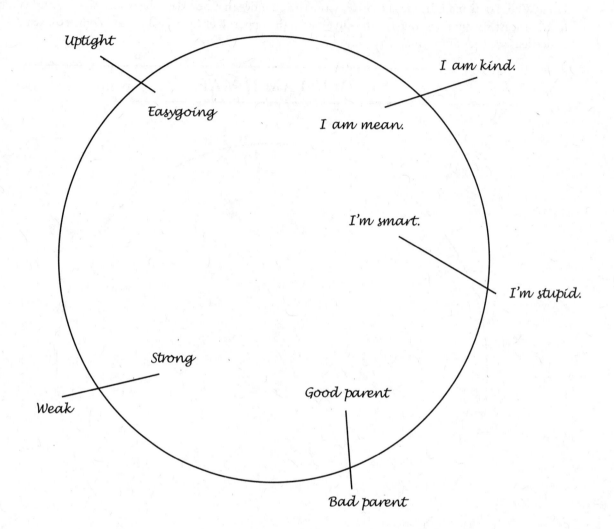

SAMPLE MAP: WHO AM I?

Uptight

Easygoing

I am kind.

I am mean.

I'm smart.

I'm stupid.

Strong

Weak

Good parent

Bad parent

1. How does each quality *inside* the circle make you feel? Describe your body tension:

_____

_____

2. Describe how you act when you feel this way:

_____

_____

3. How does each quality *outside* the circle make you feel? Describe your body tension:

_____

_____

4. Describe how you act when you feel this way:

_____

_____

5. Do the qualities inside the circle *really* describe who you are? Yes _____ No _____

6. Do the qualities outside the circle *really* describe who you are? Yes _____ No _____

Your I-System has you believing that the qualities inside the circle define you. Whenever you think you have any of the qualities outside the circle, your I-System tells you that you're lacking or damaged. Your actions then follow that feeling state. Your I-System wants to convince you that you are who you *think* you are. The qualities you listed are just thoughts about you, not you.

7. Use your bridging awareness practices and thought labeling, and review all the qualities on your map. What happens?

_____

_____

When you use your bridging awareness practices and thought labeling, you expand the circle to include everything on your map. When you aren't driven by your requirements, you are *everything*, which means you can have any quality on your map (even negative ones) without activating your I-System. When your natural self is in charge, who you are is no longer limited by your I-System. Who you are is so vast, boundless, and ever changing that your thinking mind can't grasp it. You are much greater than who you think you are. In this state of harmony and balance, you make the right choices to take care of yourself without the interference of anger.

WHO RUNS YOUR LIFE: YOU OR YOUR EMOTIONS?

When you are the CEO of your emotions, you bring harmony and balance to your daily life. You don't need a guide for how to balance love of self with love of others, or even how to handle your anger. As long as your I-System is quiet, your natural self is able to deal with the strongest emotions, such as anger, hate, greed, jealousy, shame, guilt, love, happiness, and joy. It's not about the quality or quantity of the emotion; it's simply about who's in charge: your constricted, powerless self or your expansive, natural self. No matter how true your love is or how strong your other emotions are, if your I-System is active, it will limit how you take care of yourself and your relationships.

1. Go back over your past. List three experiences where positive emotions caused you to make poor decisions, not take good care of yourself, or get angry.

Experience	Positive Emotion
Became so infatuated with my sister's friend that I missed classes and almost flunked out of college	*Love*

2. List three experiences you had where negative emotions caused you to make poor choices and not take good care of yourself.

Experience	Negative Emotion
Got really mad at my boss, kept it bottled up, and exploded at home	*Anger*

POSITIVE EMOTIONAL EXPERIENCE

1. From your prior list, select the positive emotion that caused you the most grief and write it in the oval. Take a couple of minutes to write your thoughts around the oval. Work quickly, without editing your thoughts.

> ## STRONGEST POSITIVE EMOTION MAP

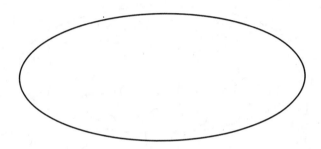

A. Is your mind cluttered or clear?

_____

B. Is your body tense or relaxed? Describe your body tension:

_____

C. Place a "D" next to each depressor thought and an "F" next to each fixer thought.

D. What are your requirements?

_____

_____

E. How do you take care of yourself in this emotional state?

_____

_____

137

2. Do this map again. Write the same positive emotion in the oval. Before you continue writing, listen to any background sounds, feel your body's pressure on your seat, sense your feet on the floor, and feel the pen in your hand. Take your time. Once you feel settled, keep feeling the pen in your hand and start writing. Watch the ink go onto the paper, and listen to any background sounds. For the next few minutes, jot down whatever thoughts pop into your mind.

STRONGEST POSITIVE EMOTION MAP WITH BRIDGING

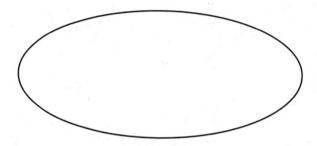

A. What are the differences between the two maps?

_____

_____

B. What anger reduction tools will you use to defuse the rest of your requirements on the first map in the exercise?

_____

_____

C. Do you see how your emotions aren't the issue, how it's your I-System?
   Yes _____ No _____

All emotions are from executive mode. When a situation arises where an emotion is grabbed by your I-System, listen to the background sounds and label your thoughts. It's also helpful to map out your requirements connected to this captured emotion. Switching off the I-System always supports health and wellness.

NEGATIVE EMOTIONAL EXPERIENCE

1. From the earlier list, select the negative emotion that caused you the most grief and write it in the oval. Write your thoughts around the oval for a couple of minutes.

STRONGEST NEGATIVE EMOTION MAP

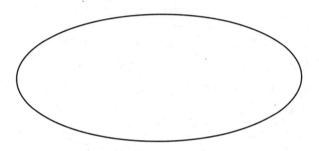

A. Is your mind cluttered or clear?

_____

B. Is your body tense or relaxed? Describe your body tension:

_____

C. Place a "D" next to each depressor thought and an "F" next to each fixer thought.

D. What are your requirements?

_____

_____

E. How do you take care of yourself in this state?

_____

2. Do this map again. Write the same negative emotion in the oval. Before you continue writing, use your bridging awareness practices. Listen to background sounds and feel your body's pressure on your seat, your feet on the floor, and the pen in your hand. Take your time. Once you are settled, keep feeling the pen in your hand as you start writing. Watch the ink go onto the paper, and listen to background sounds. For the next few minutes, jot down any thoughts that come to mind.

STRONGEST NEGATIVE EMOTION MAP WITH BRIDGING

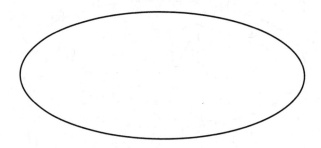

A. What are the differences between the two maps?

_____

_____

B. Is your I-System or your natural self in charge?

_____

C. What anger reduction tools will you use to defuse the rest of your requirements on the first map in the exercise?

_____

_____

D. Do you see how your emotions aren't the issue, that it's your I-System?
   Yes _____ No _____

As this map shows, your negative emotions are not your enemy. When you are in executive mode, you manage your emotions without having angry outbursts. Your natural self, functioning in executive mode, automatically results in mind-body well-being.

DO YOUR QUALITIES DEFINE OR CONFINE YOU?

Take a couple of minutes to think about your five most important qualities. Write one of your five most important qualities (for example, *trustworthy*, *hardworking*, or *loving*) inside each of the sections of the circle below. One or two words will do for each quality.

MY FIVE MOST IMPORTANT QUALITIES MAP

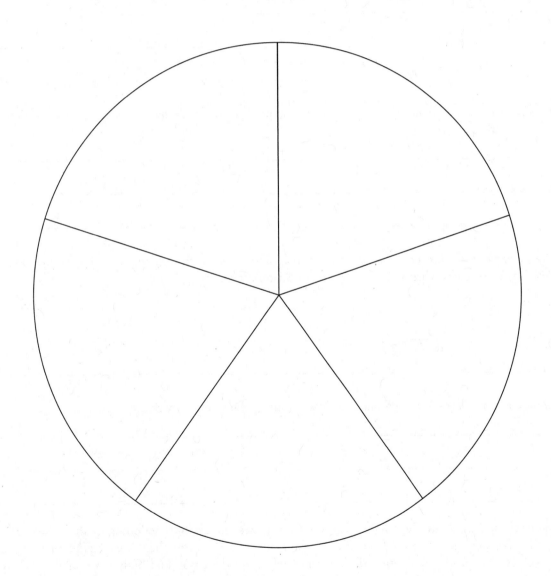

1. Look at your map and cross out the quality that's least important to you. What's your reaction as you imagine yourself without this first quality?

   _____

   _____

   _____

2. Cross out the quality that's the next least important to you. What's your reaction as you imagine yourself without this second quality?

   _____

   _____

   _____

3. Again, cross out the quality that's the next least important to you. What's your reaction as you cross out this third quality?

   _____

   _____

   _____

4. Choose between the last two qualities on your map and cross out the one that's less important to you. What's your reaction when you cross out this next-to-last quality?

   _____

   _____

   _____

5. Think about the last remaining quality. Cross it out. What's your experience now?

   _____

   _____

   _____

The levels of tension and how hard it is to cross out these naturally functioning qualities show how strongly the I-System limits you. It takes hold of your qualities and turns them into requirements. It's as if your goodness depends on meeting those requirements. Your reaction and body sensations when you were crossing out your qualities show how strongly your I-System tries to define you as a limited set of qualities. With a calm I-System, your natural self is no longer confined to a limited way of seeing yourself. In that executive functioning state, you, not your I-System, are the boss of your well-being.

SELF-CARE GOALS

Now that it's becoming clear that anger that is not managed affects your choices in life, let's see who is in charge of your self-care goals.

1. Around the oval, write your thoughts about the self-care goals you want to accomplish. Write for a couple of minutes without editing your thoughts. Describe your body tension at the bottom of the map.

SELF-CARE GOALS MAP

Body Tension: _____

A. What are your depressors?

_____

B. What are your fixers?

_____

C. What are your storylines?

_____

D. What are your requirements?

_____

E. How do you take care of yourself in this state?

_____

2. Do this map again using bridging awareness practices. Before you start writing about your self-care goals, listen to background sounds and feel your body's pressure on your seat, your feet on the floor, and the pen in your hand. Take your time. Once you are settled, keep feeling the pen in your hand as you start writing. Watch the ink go onto the paper and keep listening to background sounds. For the next few minutes, jot down any thoughts that come to mind.

SELF-CARE GOALS MAP WITH BRIDGING

SELF-CARE GOALS

A. How is this map the same as or different from the previous map?

_____

B. Are any of the items associated with body tension? Yes _____ No _____

C. For those items with body tension, do you recognize your requirements?

_____

_____

D. List the self-care goals that don't have associated body tension:

_____

_____

_____

To stop anger from influencing your health and well-being, simply quiet your I-System by defusing your requirements. In this state of wellness, you naturally take care of yourself.

DISCOVER MBB ACTION STEPS FOR SELF-CARE

1. Select one of the self-care goals listed on your previous map that was *free* of body tension. Write it in the oval. Next, take a couple of minutes to write around the oval your thoughts about what you are going to do to achieve that goal. Be specific. Describe your body tension at the bottom of the map.

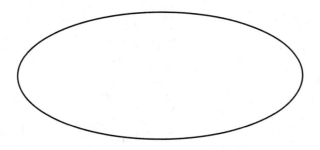

SELF-CARE GOAL ACHIEVEMENT MAP

Body Tension: _____

A. What are your depressors?

_____

B. What are your fixers?

_____

C. What are your storylines?

_____

D. What are your requirements?

_____

_____

Did you see how your I-System grabbed a goal that used to be without body tension, created requirements about reaching your goal, and limited your success? Your active I-System will always create trouble and clutter your path to success.

2. Do this map again using bridging awareness practices. Write the same topic in the oval. Before you start writing about how you are going to achieve that goal, listen to background sounds and feel your body's pressure on your seat, your feet on the floor, and the pen in your hand. Take your time. Once you are settled, keep feeling the pen in your hand as you start writing. Watch the ink go onto the paper and keep listening to background sounds. Write for a couple of minutes.

SELF-CARE GOAL ACHIEVEMENT MAP WITH BRIDGING

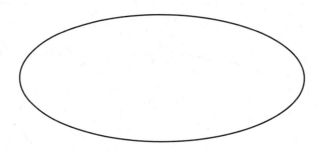

A. Circle those items *without* body tension. These are possible action steps.

B. Choose three of these items as the MBB action steps you want to take for stress- and anger-free self-care. List them:

_____

_____

_____

Use this two-part mapping process to separate the I-System's action steps from the MBB action steps you discover while you are in executive mode (bridging awareness map). Remember, the items on your bridging awareness map that come without body tension and mind clutter are all MBB action steps that you could take. For success, you need to do each action step with a quiet I-System. If body tension and mind clutter arise when you are doing your action steps, use your anger reduction tools to quiet your I-System. With the I-System no longer in charge of your actions, your choices now come from your executive mode, and the MBB action steps are done by your natural self.

NOW IS THE ONLY TIME YOU CAN TAKE CARE OF YOURSELF

1. Do a Past, Present, and Future map. In the "Past" section of this map, take a couple of minutes to jot down whatever comes to mind about your past. Then describe your body tension. Next, in the "Future" section of this map, take another couple of minutes to write whatever comes to mind about your future. Describe your body tension. Finally, in the "Present" section of this map, take a couple of minutes to jot down whatever comes to mind about the present and, again, describe your body tension.

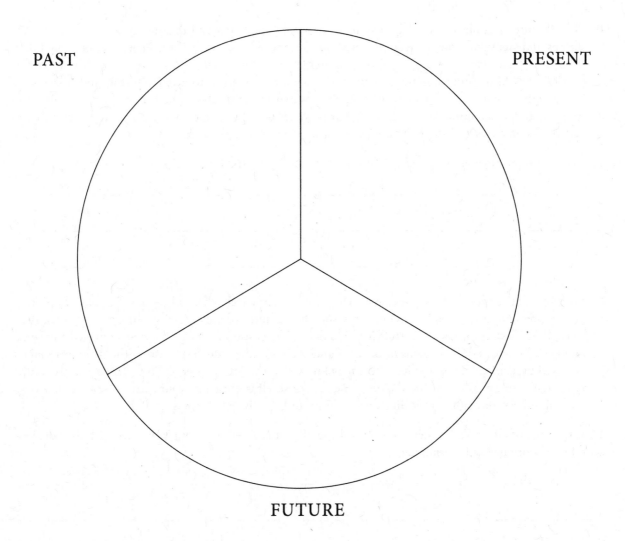

PAST, PRESENT, AND FUTURE MAP

PAST

PRESENT

FUTURE

Let's think about this remarkable map:

A. The "Past" section of your map is full of storylines with themes like *My childhood was bad, I made it through by sheer willpower* and *My friends always supported me.* True or not, positive or negative, these stories create mind clutter; they tense your body and take you away from the present. When you recognize storylines in real time, notice that they take you away from doing what you need to do in the present.

What do you notice about the "Past" section of your map? List your storylines:

_____

_____

_____

B. The "Future" section of your map may have many of your hopes and dreams. Beside each item that brings body tension, write the requirements you can find. For instance, if the item that's creating body tension is *I won't give in to my anger*, the requirement is *I should not give in to my anger*. The I-System has taken hold of your naturally functioning thought, turned it into a requirement, and filled your body with tension and your mind with clutter. When thoughts about the future that are driven by the I-System come up in real time, note your body tension, find your requirements, and use bridging awareness practices and thought labeling to bring you back to the present.

List the requirements you notice on the "Future" section of your map:

_____

_____

_____

C. The "Present" section of this map shows what you currently feel and think. Look for signs of an over-active I-System, such as body tension, depressors, fixers, and storylines. Can you uncover your requirements? The I-System has taken stuff from your past and future to try to fix your damaged image of yourself. Look carefully for signs of the fixer and then find the hidden depressor. The depressor makes you feel broken and drives the fixer. You now know that the fixer can never "fix" the damage, because you aren't broken. You don't need fixing. The damaged self is caused by your active I-System, not what you have been through, and it limits your ability to fully live in the present.

List any signs of an active I-System you find in the "Present" section of your map. Also list your depressors, fixers, storylines, and requirements:

_____

_____

_____

2. Do a Present map. Before you start writing about the present, use your bridging awareness practices. Listen to background sounds and feel your body's pressure on your seat, your feet on the floor, and the pen in your hand. Take your time. Once you are settled, keep feeling the pen in your hand as you start writing any thoughts that come to mind about the present. Watch the ink go onto the paper and keep listening to background sounds.

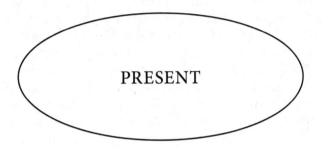

| PRESENT MAP WITH BRIDGING |

A. What do you notice about this map that's different from the "Present" section of your Past, Present, and Future map?

_____

_____

B. Note how you would take care of yourself and your responsibilities in this mind-body state:

_____

_____

Being in the present is not being in a zone, nor is it a moment of enlightenment or a magical state of being. Your natural self is always present right here, right now. When your I-System is calm, you are in the present, where your anger is well managed. Requirements take you away from your natural self that is living right here, right now. If your depressor has you feeling *not good enough*, *bored*, *overwhelmed*, *lacking*, or *hopeless*, you have a hidden requirement that's pulling you down and taking over your natural executive functioning. On the other hand, when your fixer has you feeling *pushed* and *irritated*, and as if *enough is never enough*, you have a hidden requirement that's also taking over your executive functioning. When your I-System is in high gear, look for your hidden requirement and use bridging awareness practices to come back to the present moment and do what you need to do right now.

PUTTING IT ALL TOGETHER

Bruce, a diabetic, was in a residential treatment facility for chronic alcoholism. He had poor impulse control and a long history of angry outbursts, including bar fights, and rash decisions. When his wife called to tell him that his son was in trouble, Bruce hung up the phone in anger and chose to leave the program right away, even though his treatment was not finished. As he began packing his clothes, he remembered his bridging awareness practices. Bruce felt the fabric of his clothes, heard the sound of the air conditioner, and (without any prodding from the staff) unpacked his suitcase. He called his wife, and they began planning how to help their son. In group he explained how a sense of clarity about his life came into his mind as he came to his senses. Mapping showed that his requirement for his son (He shouldn't get into trouble) had switched on his I-System and that his fixer had led him to impulsive actions and rash choices, like packing his clothes and starting to leave. With his expanded awareness, Bruce was able to take care of himself and his family calmly, with his natural self in charge.

When your I-System is in control of your self-care, your ability to take care of yourself and meet your responsibilities is restricted and confined. Your choices become limited by the dance of the depressor and fixer. The blinders of your I-System limit how you think, act, and see yourself and the world. The natural harmony of your mind-body is disrupted, anger takes center stage, and your health suffers.

When you use your anger reduction tools, your natural self, in executive mode, is in charge of your self-care. With a clearer mind and calmer body, your decisions about your self-care are natural and the choices become clear. A unified mind-body state goes hand in hand with wellness.

Anger Reduction Tools

➤ Defuse requirements to allow proper self-care and support wellness.

➤ Uncover and use MBB action steps for self-care and wellness.

MBB Rating Scale

Stop Anger from Interfering with Your Health and Well-Being

Date: _____

After using the tools in this chapter for a few days, check the box that best describes your practice: hardly ever, sometimes, usually, almost always.

How often do you...	Hardly Ever	Sometimes	Usually	Almost Always
Know when your health and wellness are driven by your I-System?				
Notice when you are taking care of yourself naturally, with an I-System at rest?				
Have positive emotions with a quiet I-System?				
Have negative emotions with a quiet I-System?				
Defuse requirements that get in the way of your self-care?				
Experience and express your natural self in the present moment?				
Follow through with self-care MBB action steps?				
Notice that wellness and a quiet I-System go hand in hand?				

List three situations where your I-System got in the way of your ability to care for yourself:

_____

_____

_____

List the requirements that you were able to defuse associated with the situations above:

_____

_____

_____

List three self-care MBB action steps you are taking to ensure wellness:

_____

_____

_____

CHAPTER 8

REDUCE CONFLICTS

Principles

An I-System that is active (on) creates turmoil in your relationships.

An I-System at rest (off) reduces conflicts.

CONFLICT REDUCTION

Every day, we find ourselves in situations where conflicts with those around us can happen. These situations may involve how we see an event, how we emotionally experience something, how we process what's happening, or how we react. When the event does not switch on the I-System of either party, the natural self of each person is able to work out those differences without harmful outcomes. When the event switches on each person's I-System, a major conflict is bound to happen. Then the way each person sees and responds depends on his or her set of requirements. Rather than each person trying to resolve the conflict, there is a clash of I-Systems, and it becomes almost impossible to resolve their differences. Angry exchanges then follow as the depressor/fixer cycle gains control, and verbal or physical conflicts often result.

Max, a well-known elected official, seemed to have his life on an even keel except for his relationship with his teenage daughter, Sue. For example, one day Max came home after a long day of work and asked Sue how she was doing. Sue promptly responded, "None of your business." Getting red in the face, Max motioned to Sue with his fist, walked to the door, and slammed it on his way out. Afraid that he would slap Sue next time, he began mind-body bridging. The turning point was Max's recognition that his expectations for proper behavior became I-System requirements that were keeping him from dealing with Sue in his usual, steady fashion. Once Max defused his requirements for his daughter (*She should be nice to me*, *She should obey the house rules*), his body became calm and he was able to relate to Sue in a way that helped her to improve her behavior at home.

Conflict involves two parties clashing and sharply disagreeing; however, when your I-System is calm, even if the other party is unyielding, your involvement in the conflict ceases. Because your I-System is quiet, there is only one party in conflict. The other person is limited in his or her choices, but your options for courses of action are wide open.

To reduce conflicts that come up in your life, it is critical to be clearly aware of and in control of your I-System. With an I-System at rest, your natural self, in executive mode, leads you to make the right decisions, without letting your angry emotions or behavior complicate the matter. Even if the other party is rigid and won't compromise, you can be assured that with a quiet I-System, you are making proper choices. In the executive loop, you gain confidence in your position without needing to rely on angry or harmful behavior.

EMOTIONS INFLUENCE CONFLICT

1. Think about an important relationship and note what emotion (other than anger) is involved when you have a conflict with that person. In the oval, write that emotion (for example: *jealousy*, *envy*, *greed*, *guilt*, *sadness*, *depression*, or *love*). Around the oval, write your thoughts about that emotion for a couple of minutes, without editing them. At the bottom of the map, describe your body tension and its location.

EMOTION MAP

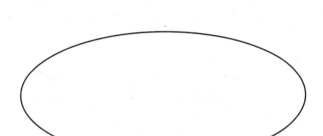

Body Tension and Location: _____

A. What is your depressor/fixer doing?

_____

_____

B. Identify and list as many requirements as you can:

_____

_____

_____

C. How do you act in this state?

_____

When emotions come with body tension and mind clutter, the I-System is switched on, making it very tough to reduce conflicts.

2. Do the map again, writing the same emotion in the oval. Before you start writing, listen to background sounds and feel your body's pressure on your seat, your feet on the floor, and the pen in your hand. Take your time. Once you are settled, keep feeling the pen in your hand as you start writing. Watch the ink go onto the paper and listen to background sounds. For the next few minutes, jot down any thoughts that come to mind.

EMOTION MAP WITH BRIDGING

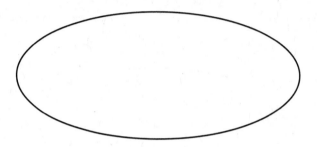

What's your mind-body state after bridging, and how do you act in this state?

_____

_____

Emotions, like thoughts, are from executive functioning until the I-System grabs them. Every single emotion you will ever have comes from your reservoir of natural functioning. When the I-System takes hold of that emotion, it either adds to it (*so guilty that I can't sleep, can't take care of my responsibilities*) or takes away from it (*so numb to guilt that I keep taking advantage of others*).

During the day, when your emotions seem to be getting the best of you, use your bridging awareness practices and thought labeling, and then recognize the two parts of emotions: *thoughts* and *body sensations*. Breaking down an emotion (*jealousy*) into thoughts (*Why did he get the promotion? I don't like him*) and body sensations (*tight fist, chest pressure*) reduces the power the emotion has over you. As you have learned from your bridging map, a calmer mind and body allow you to experience your emotions without the heat of your I-System. This puts your natural self in the driver's seat.

OVERCOME UNSETTLING EVENTS WITH FAMILY (PARTNER)

1. Throughout the day, notice unsettling events with family that create conflict. Fill in the chart below.

Unsettling Event	Your Reaction	Requirement
My partner criticized my cooking.	*Yelled, threw the food away, and smashed the plate.*	*My partner shouldn't criticize my cooking.*
On family game night, my brother won and called me a loser.	*Got angry and stormed out of the room.*	*My brother shouldn't call me a loser.*
My father took my car keys after I came home late.	*Told him I hated him and that it was my car, not his.*	*My father shouldn't take my keys.*

2. Describe your body tension and its progression for the three events that disturbed you the most:

_____

_____

_____

3. Do you see how your I-System, not the events, creates havoc in your daily life?
   Yes _____ No _____

4. Now, from your previous list, choose the most unsettling event and write it in the oval. Write your thoughts around the oval for a couple of minutes without editing them.

UNSETTLING EVENT WITH FAMILY (PARTNER) MAP

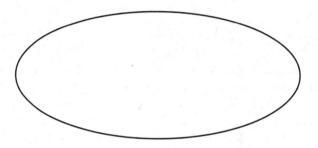

A. What is your body tension, and how does it progress?

_____

B. List your depressor/fixer storylines:

_____

_____

C. Identify and list as many requirements as you can:

_____

_____

_____

D. How is your I-System keeping you from an appropriate resolution?

_____

_____

Anger is a natural emotion from executive functioning that prepares you for appropriate action. Remember that emotions have two parts: a thought and a body sensation. When the I-System grabs your anger, it makes you feel that you can't cope. Then your anger builds into explosive and harmful outbursts that stop you from being able to resolve the conflict.

5. Do this map again, writing the same unsettling event in the oval. Before you continue writing, listen to background sounds and feel your body's pressure on your seat, your feet on the floor, and the pen in your hand. Take your time. Once you are settled, keep feeling the pen in your hand as you start writing. Watch the ink go onto the paper and listen to background sounds. For the next few minutes, jot down any thoughts that come to mind.

UNSETTLING EVENT WITH FAMILY (PARTNER) MAP WITH BRIDGING

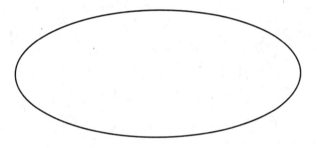

A. What's your mind-body state on this map, compared to the previous one?

_____

_____

B. How would you act differently in this state?

_____

_____

C. Do you think you can defuse your requirements from the previous map next time the situation comes up? Yes _____ No _____

D. What anger reduction tools will you use?

_____

When you calm your I-System and defuse your requirements, you control how you react and your natural self can deal with conflict.

OVERCOME UNSETTLING EVENTS AT WORK AND WITH FRIENDS

1. Throughout the day, notice unsettling events at work and with friends that created conflict. Fill in the chart below.

Unsettling Event	Your Reaction	Requirement
My best friend, Lisa, talked about me behind my back.	Didn't talk to her for months.	Lisa shouldn't talk about me.
Tom keeps bragging about his successes.	Made fun of him and tried to put him in his place.	Tom shouldn't brag.
Got fired at work.	Stunned, pissed off, I was angry at everyone for weeks.	I shouldn't be fired.

The first step in dealing with a conflict is to notice the first signs of an I-System that's switched on: body tension and mind clutter. Next, use your favorite bridging awareness practice (such as listening to background sounds or rubbing your fingers together) and find your requirement. To defuse a requirement, please remember that it's not the situation or even how competitive you are about it that is causing your angry reactions; it's your hidden requirement. Some requirements are easy to defuse, but if the requirement you are working with is hard to defuse, know that there may be other, related requirements you haven't found yet. When you don't defuse your requirement, it always has the power to create anger and resentment. Doing maps like the following ones will help.

2. Write in the oval the most unsettling event from the prior chart where your I-System was in control. Around the oval, write your thoughts for a couple of minutes without editing them. Describe your body tension at the bottom of the map.

MOST UNSETTLING EVENT AT WORK AND WITH FRIENDS MAP

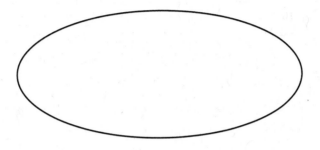

A. What is your body tension, and how does it progress?

_____

B. List your depressor and fixer storylines:

_____

_____

C. Identify and list as many requirements as you can:

_____

_____

_____

D. How is your I-System keeping you from an appropriate resolution?

_____

_____

3. Do the previous map again, writing the same event in the oval. Before you continue writing, listen to background sounds and feel your body's pressure on your seat, your feet on the floor, and the pen in your hand. Take your time. Once you are settled, keep feeling the pen in your hand as you start writing. Watch the ink go onto the paper and listen to background sounds. For the next few minutes, jot down any thoughts that come to mind.

MOST UNSETTLING EVENT AT WORK AND WITH FRIENDS MAP WITH BRIDGING

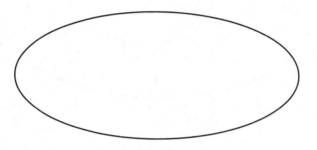

A. What's your mind-body state on this map, compared to the previous map?

_____

_____

B. How would you act differently if you were in this state?

_____

_____

C. Do you see that your work and relationships with others can be greatly improved when you calm your I-System? Yes _____ No _____

D. Describe how you will recognize and defuse your requirements in real time:

_____

_____

REDUCE CONFLICT

1. List some heated conflicts you have had over the past few weeks:

Conflict Issue	Conflict Outcome	Requirement
Mary went shopping and spent $750 on stuff we didn't need.	*I confronted her; she tried to justify it; I got really angry, yelled, and called her dirty names.*	*Mary shouldn't spend so much money.*

2. For each conflict outcome, describe your storylines and the roles of your depressor and fixer:

Storyline	Depressor	Fixer
She always wants to spend money; she thinks it grows on trees!	*We are too poor.*	*I'll make sure she doesn't do it again; I'll just cancel her credit card.*

3. From the previous chart, choose the most heated conflict. Write it in the oval. Next, write your thoughts around the oval for a couple of minutes without editing them. Describe your body tension at the bottom of the map.

HEATED CONFLICT MAP

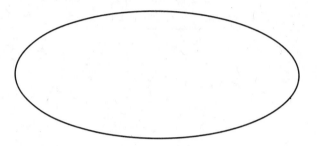

A. What is your body tension, and how does it progress?

_____

B. How does your depressor/fixer cycle keep the conflict going?

_____

_____

C. Describe the role your storylines play in your conflict:

_____

D. What are your additional requirements?

_____

E. How do you act in this state?

_____

4. Now do a bridging map about that same heated conflict. Write that conflict in the oval below. Before you continue writing, listen to any background sounds, feel your body's pressure on your seat, sense your feet on the floor, and feel the pen in your hand. Take your time. Once you feel settled, keep feeling the pen in your hand, and start writing. Watch the ink go onto the paper, and listen to any background sounds. For the next few minutes, jot down whatever thoughts pop into your mind.

HEATED CONFLICT MAP WITH BRIDGING

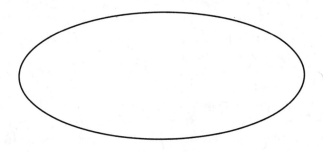

A. Is your mind cluttered or clear?

_____

B. Is your body tense or relaxed?

_____

C. How do you act in this mind-body state?

_____

D. Are you beginning to understand that your active I-System keeps the conflict unresolved?
    Yes _____ No _____

    Your anger reduction tools help you deal with any situation that comes up in your life.

165

FIVE MBB STEPS FOR CONFLICT REDUCTION

1. When you start having a difference of opinion with someone, notice your body tension and use your bridging awareness practices to calm your active I-System. Building body tension means that you are heading down a slippery slope.

2. If your mind starts to clutter with angry thoughts, keep using your bridging awareness practices and label your thoughts as just thoughts. Recall that mind clutter is the depressor/fixer cycle, and your storylines keep your I-System going.

3. Know that in all conflicts, there is a battle between each person's fixer. Each person's fixer will try to gain an advantage over the other person's fixer, by trying to stir up his or her depressor. You cannot resolve your conflict with the other person by stirring up his or her depressor with your angry attacks. Your awareness of both your depressor and your fixer will help you to defuse both of them, and put you in a position to deal with the situation while functioning in executive mode.

4. If your I-System is still on, find the requirements that switched on your I-System. It's helpful to look for all those "shoulds" and "should nots." Remember, it's not the issues involved in the conflict or the other person's actions; it's your requirements that keep you from reducing the conflict. Your I-System stays active when you embrace drama, conflict, and turmoil.

5. When you have recognized and defused your requirements, and your natural self is in charge, you are resolving *your* internal conflict. You don't have any control over the other person's I-System and what it's doing. The point is that when your I-System is quiet and your natural self is functioning in executive mode, you have the power to make proper choices in the moment. Your ability to reduce interpersonal conflicts moves to a new level.

When you use your anger reduction tools, you reduce your part in the conflict. When you function in executive mode, you give the other party time and space to settle down so that the conflict has a chance to be resolved. Even if the other party is unmoved, when you are in executive mode, you know that you have defused your requirements and have ended your part in the heated conflict. With the clarity of your natural self, you are able to choose a proper course of action.

Alice, a busy flight attendant, had no history of angry behavior until she began working with Jane. For some reason, the two never got along. Jane, who had more seniority, always made fun of Alice in front of the other attendants. Jane used a distinctive tone of voice when speaking to Alice and had a special set of behaviors for her. The final blowup came just as they were about to leave the plane after a long flight. Jane, using her special voice, said, "You smell like you had a hard day, dearie." Alice pushed Jane in response and was suspended from her job. To become reinstated, she was required to take an anger management class. Alice was referred to mind-body bridging, and after several weeks she was able to recognize her requirements regarding Jane. She successfully learned to use the Five MBB Steps for Conflict Reduction to manage her anger. Alice's natural self, functioning in executive mode, is now able to work with Jane in a professional manner.

DISCOVER YOUR MBB ACTION STEPS FOR REDUCING CONFLICT

1. It's time to discover action steps to help you reduce conflict. Choose the relationship that you most want to improve and write that person's name in the oval. Next, take a couple of minutes to write around the oval your thoughts on what you are going do to reduce conflict with that person. Be specific. Describe your body tension at the bottom of the map.

REDUCING CONFLICT MAP

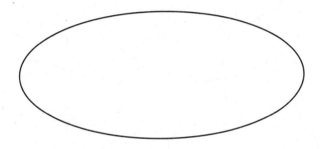

Body Tension: _____

A. What are your depressors?

_____

B. What are your fixers?

_____

C. What are your storylines?

_____

D. What are your requirements?

_____

E. Your requirements are the obstacle that prevents conflict reduction. Can you defuse them?
    Yes _____ No _____

2. Do this map again using bridging awareness practices. Write the same name in the oval. Before you start writing about what you are going to do to reduce conflict with that person, listen to background sounds and feel your body's pressure on your seat, your feet on the floor, and the pen in your hand. Take your time. Once you are settled, keep feeling the pen in your hand as you start writing. Watch the ink go onto the paper and keep listening to background sounds. For the next few minutes, write any thoughts that come to mind.

REDUCING CONFLICT MAP WITH BRIDGING

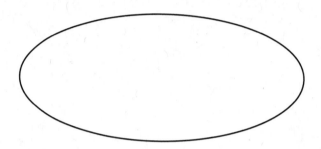

A. Circle those items *without* body tension. These are possible action steps.

B. Choose three of those items as the MBB action steps you want to take to achieve conflict reduction. List them below and begin implementing them.

_____

_____

_____

Remember that the items on this map with *no* associated body tension and mind clutter are all possible MBB action steps. To be effective, the MBB action steps must be carried out with a calm I-System. Use the two-part mapping process every day to navigate through life in executive mode.

PUTTING IT ALL TOGETHER

Mark and his brother-in-law, Sam, were always arguing about one thing or another. Family gatherings were frequent, and Mark felt that it was Sam's fault that they didn't get along. He blamed Sam for finding ways to, as he put it, "pull my chain, no matter how nice I am." After the last family get-together, their exchanges heated to a physical level, where they were pushing and shoving each other. Because the family was starting to take sides and she was afraid of what might happen next, Mark's wife made it clear that Mark needed to do something about it. Of course, Mark blamed Sam, stating, "He is the one who started it, and he needs treatment, lots of it," but Mark finally agreed to go to a mind-body bridging class.

When he was mapping, Mark found his requirements: *Sam shouldn't criticize my job*, *Sam shouldn't call me Marko Polo*, and *Sam should back off*. Once Mark's I-System was active, his depressor made him feel hurt and disrespected. His fixer would then respond with names and comments about how Sam looked, building to the point where Mark exploded into pushing and shoving his smaller brother-in-law. After using his anger reduction tools (especially the Five MBB Steps for Conflict Reduction), Mark began to see that it was not Sam who was making him a victim, but his I-System and its requirements causing him to feel hurt and vulnerable. Mark realized that it didn't make sense that Sam's name-calling and demeaning remarks caused him to get into a fight. He saw how his depressor/fixer cycle worked and was able to greatly lessen its effect.

Mark reported on the next family get-together: "I didn't take his bait, and it was really interesting that Sam did his best to aggravate me. But I was calm, cool, and collected with my natural self in charge. After that, I didn't quite know what happened, but I saw how his face was tight and tense, and I suddenly asked him about his job and we sort of got along okay. I still don't really like Sam, but ever since I calmed my I-System, the conflict has dissolved. He might still joke about me, but it doesn't bother me anymore, and sometimes he says something interesting. Also, Mary and I are closer than ever before."

When both parties have different opinions and heated I-Systems, the results are often an unresolved conflict with hurt feelings, angry outbursts, and guilt. When the other person's I-System is rigid, it's vital that you quiet your I-System so that you can deal with that situation in executive mode. As with Mark, when your natural self stays in control of your actions, you relate to the other person in a way that can change the situation, reducing the conflict.

Anger Reduction Tools

➢ Use the Five MBB Steps for Conflict Reduction.

➢ Uncover and use MBB action steps to reduce conflicts.

MBB RATING SCALE
REDUCE CONFLICTS

Date: _____

After using the tools in this chapter for a few days, check the box that best describes your practice: hardly ever, sometimes, usually, almost always.

How often do you...	Hardly Ever	Sometimes	Usually	Almost Always
Notice when your I-System has taken hold of a situation, creating conflict?				
Defuse requirements that add to the conflict?				
Defuse requirements that stir up your emotions?				
Defuse requirements about the conflict?				
Use the Five MBB Steps for Conflict Reduction?				
Put into place and follow your MBB action steps for reducing conflict?				
Feel confident about your future?				

List three requirements you have defused:

_____

_____

_____

List three examples of how you used your anger reduction tools to change your life:

_____

_____

_____

List what action steps you have taken and how they went:

_____

_____

CHAPTER 9

MANAGE ANGER
ANYTIME, ANYPLACE

Principles

An I-System that is switched on will never stop filling your life with anger.

When you switch off your I-System, you are able to manage your anger and face any challenge confidently with your natural self, in executive mode.

FACING DIFFICULT SITUATIONS

The future is often uncertain and unpredictable. We don't have control over what the future has in store for us. What you do have control over is who is in charge, your I-System or your natural self. When the I-System is in the driver's seat, challenges become crises as you are filled with a sense of powerlessness. Angry outbursts are then likely to occur. By making your anger reduction tools a part of your daily life, even when you face a full-blown crisis, you have the ability to do so in executive mode, with your natural self making the best choices.

Shirley, a retired army nurse, couldn't stand the "slow pace" of civilian life. In a fast-food restaurant, she would get annoyed and angry when the line wouldn't move fast enough. When a traffic light turned green and the car in front of her didn't move forward right away, she would honk the horn over and over while making obscene gestures. In her work as a unit nursing supervisor, her staff could never think or move quickly enough to satisfy her. When golfing with her friends, Shirley was fiercely competitive and was always pushing herself to reduce her low handicap. She also suffered a lot of injuries from skiing in conditions beyond her abilities, and chalked those injuries up to, as she put it, "That's just who I am."

Shirley was given a mind-body bridging workbook by a fellow golfer to help her improve her game. After starting the book, she noticed right away that she slept better and was less irritable. After she did a number of maps, her "aha" moment came when she clearly saw the power of her depressor. Her Competition map showed that behind her drive to be first was her fixer trying to fix the bad feelings her depressor caused. From her Reducing Conflict map with Bridging, she discovered her MBB action steps. They surprised her, because she realized that she could enjoy each step along the way even if she didn't reach a major goal: "I am worth something even when I achieve nothing." This newfound knowledge gave her the satisfaction she had never had before. Her relationship with her friends improved, her angry outbursts reduced, she was given more responsibilities at work, and, to her amazement, her golf handicap went down.

By mapping a number of tough situations that often lead to a crisis, this chapter brings together all your anger reduction tools so that you can effectively handle any challenge that comes up in life. Also in this chapter, you will learn an advanced, rapid-fire mapping practice to find your hidden requirements, called *power mapping*. This free-association tool quickly expands your awareness of your requirements about a problem, situation, event, or person. Without using your bridging awareness practices, you do map after map, just watching your switched-on I-System in action. When you power map, your I-System has free rein, but at the same time, your natural self is still in the driver's seat. When you make a habit of power mapping, you can experience firsthand that no matter how intense your anger is, you can always be in control with your natural self in the driver's seat.

COMPETITION

When your I-System takes hold of your natural competitive spirit, it corrupts your ambitions and distorts your drive to excel. Your success is now being pushed by the I-System and its fixer. A competitive game turns into a battle where no prisoners are taken, losing ten pounds becomes a do-or-die struggle, and money equals self-worth. Since your depressor drains your self-esteem, no competition will ever make you feel like a winner. Your aggressive and assertive spirit is now filled with anger that is directed both inward and outward.

1. Think back to when you were competitive with others or yourself, and how you reacted when things became heated. Recognize your underlying requirements.

Competitive Situation	Your Reaction	Requirements
I beat Lisa at darts.	*Posted it on Facebook and bragged to everyone.*	*I should win.*
Tom got the account.	*Stormed out of the building and went to the nearest bar.*	*I should have gotten the account.*
I missed that eight-foot putt.	*Broke my putter and threw it into the lake.*	*I should always make that putt.*

The first step in dealing with a competitive situation is to notice the early signs of an I-System that's active, like body tension and storylines about fears of losing or the urgent pressure to win. If you do, use your favorite bridging awareness practice (such as listening to background sounds or rubbing your fingers together), and then recognize and defuse any requirements. Remember that it's not the situation or even your competitive nature that is causing your angry reactions; it's your requirements. Once recognized, some requirements are easy to defuse, but if the requirement is hard to defuse, realize that there are other, related requirements that you haven't found yet. When you don't defuse your requirement, it always has the power to create anger and resentment when you don't win. Even if you do win, that requirement has kept you from competing at your best.

2. From the prior list, choose the competitive situation that created the most tension and angry reaction. Write it in the oval. Around the oval, write your thoughts about this situation for a couple of minutes, without editing them.

COMPETITION MAP

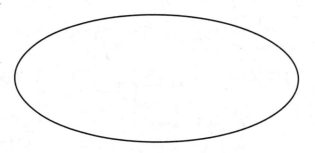

A. List your body tension and its progression:

_____

B. What are your depressor and fixer doing?

_____

_____

C. Identify and list as many requirements as you can:

_____

_____

_____

_____

D. How do you act in this state?

_____

Even if you win, the requirements on this map that are not defused will limit your performance.

3. Do the map again, writing the same competitive situation in the oval. Before you continue writing, listen to background sounds and feel your body's pressure on your seat, your feet on the floor, and the pen in your hand. Take your time. Once you are settled, keep feeling the pen in your hand as you start writing. Watch the ink go onto the paper and listen to background sounds. For the next few minutes, jot down any thoughts that come to mind.

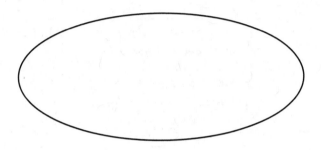

COMPETITION MAP WITH BRIDGING

A. What's your mind-body state after bridging, and how do you act in this state?

_____

_____

B. How are you going to defuse the remaining requirements on your prior map?

_____

_____

Win, lose, or draw, defusing requirements means that you win by having your natural self, in executive mode, in the driver's seat.

STAY CALM WHEN THE BOTTOM FALLS OUT

1. We have all had situations where we felt comfortable that everything was under control and then someone else's behavior suddenly caused the bottom to fall out. Fill out the chart below, and list some of those situations.

Troubling Situation	Your Reaction	Requirement
Martha didn't keep her promise.	*Angrily told her to go to hell.*	*Martha should keep her promise.*
Marvin lied.	*Called him names, threw the lamp at him, and stormed out.*	*Marvin should tell the truth.*
Our son didn't follow the rules, and associates with drug dealers.	*Yelled, pleaded, felt helpless, considered calling the police.*	*He should follow the rules and shouldn't associate with drug dealers.*

It's crucial to be aware of when you first start to worry that you are losing control in a situation. When you use your anger reduction tools right away, you will stop your I-System from being boss and will keep angry outbursts and abuse from happening.

2. From the prior chart, choose the most troubling situation where you lost control. Write that situation in the oval. Around the oval, write your thoughts for a couple of minutes without editing them.

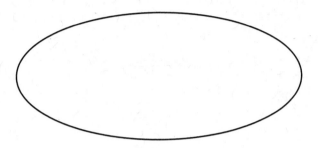

LOSING CONTROL MAP

A. What is your body tension, and how does it progress?

_____

B. List your depressor/fixer storylines:

_____

_____

C. Identify and list as many requirements as you can:

_____

_____

_____

D. Describe how you act in this state:

_____

_____

3. Do the map again, writing the same troubling situation in the oval. Before you continue writing, listen to background sounds and feel your body's pressure on your seat, your feet on the floor, and the pen in your hand. Take your time. Once you are settled, keep feeling the pen in your hand as you start writing. Watch the ink go onto the paper and listen to background sounds. For the next few minutes, jot down any thoughts that come to mind.

LOSING CONTROL MAP WITH BRIDGING

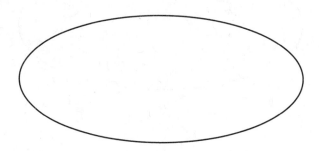

A. What's your mind-body state after bridging, and how do you act in this state?

_____

_____

B. How did your attempt to defuse your remaining requirements go?

_____

_____

Remember, for those requirements that are hard to defuse, find and break down the large requirement into smaller ones. For example, take the requirement *My kids should behave*. You know what your requirement is, but you're having trouble defusing it. So ask yourself, *What does that requirement look like?* For example, *They should not leave their bikes in the driveway*, *They should be grateful for everything they get*, *They should listen to me*, *They shouldn't fight with each other*, *They should do their chores*, *They shouldn't talk back to me*, *They shouldn't always want things*. These more detailed requirements are easier to work with and defuse. When you defuse them, the requirement that was hard to defuse (*My kids should behave*) will defuse on its own.

NOT ENOUGH

Our I-System keeps comparing us to others. It tells us (by creating requirements about how we and the world should be) that we don't have enough of *something* (money, smarts, looks, education, or connections), resulting in envy and jealousy. Caught by the rules of the I-System, we respond with anger and improper behavior.

1. Think about a situation where you didn't have enough time, money, energy, attractiveness, talent, and so on that still brings up anger, body tension, and mind clutter. Now fill out the chart below.

Situation	Your Reaction	Requirement
Didn't have enough time to study for final exam.	Got angry at the whole system; dropped the course.	I should have more time to study.
Lou bought a BMW sports coupe that I can't afford.	When I saw the car, I was furious, didn't go home, went to the pub, and drank too much.	I should be the one who could afford that kind of car.
Mary got a date with the new doctor in town.	Called her a social climber in front of our friends.	I should be the one he asked out.

As long as your requirements are not defused, your I-System will rule your life and create bitterness and jealousy. It is not what the other person has or what he or she is doing that is creating your difficulties; it's your I-System. The following maps will clarify the situation for you.

2. From the previous chart, choose the most difficult situation and write it in the oval below. Next, around the oval, write your thoughts about the situation. Write for a couple of minutes.

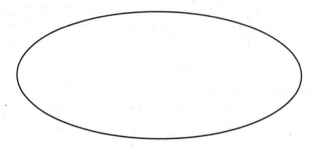

NOT ENOUGH MAP

A. What is your body tension, and how does it progress?

_____

B. What are your depressors?

_____

C. What are your fixers?

_____

D. What are your storylines?

_____

E. List your requirements:

_____

_____

F. How do you act in this mind-body state?

_____

3. Do this map again using bridging awareness practices. Write the same difficult situation in the oval. Before you continue writing, listen to background sounds and feel your body's pressure on your seat, your feet on the floor, and the pen in your hand. Take your time. Once you are settled, keep feeling the pen in your hand as you start writing. Watch the ink go onto the paper and keep listening to background sounds. For the next few minutes, jot down any thoughts that come to mind about the situation.

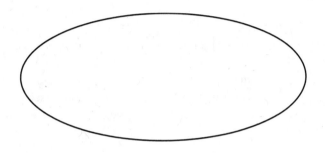

| NOT ENOUGH MAP WITH BRIDGING |

A. What do you notice that is different on this map?

_____

B. How do you act with a quiet I-System?

_____

C. How will you defuse your requirements on the previous map when the situation arises again?

_____

_____

After doing the bridging map, if you still have body tension and feel you may have a hard time when the situation comes up again, use the following information about power mapping to find those stubbornly hidden requirements. Power mapping is only for people who have had success with using mindbody bridging practices in their daily lives. Use power mapping when your overactive I-System is hard to handle, such as when you have anger issues that are not resolved or are ready to explode.

POWER MAP YOUR WAY OUT OF ANGER

Power mapping is a great tool, but it only works for those who have a solid foundation of mind-body bridging practices and have had success in recognizing and defusing requirements. It is important to have at least twenty to thirty minutes of time to yourself when you power map.

1. To power map, sit down with a pen and pad of paper. In the center of the paper, write the issue that troubles you the most (for example, *My partner had an affair*). Draw an oval around that issue and quickly jot down whatever thoughts come to mind. Let your I-System run wild as you write. Don't use your bridging awareness practices, don't try to reduce your anger, and don't try to solve the issue. All you have to do is watch your I-System in action. When you have completed the map, write down your body tension at the bottom of the page.

2. Now take the most troubling thought from the map you just did, write it in an oval on another piece of paper, and begin mapping that thought. When you finish, write down your body tension at the bottom of the page. Repeat this process by taking the most troubling thought on one map and making it the topic of the next map. Make map after map after map. Map for as long as it takes, until your I-System quiets and your anger naturally subsides. Look over your maps for requirements you were not previously aware of. Those requirements were switching on your I-System and fueling your anger.

3. Review your series of maps and note how your body tension eventually reduces as your anger recedes. It's not possible to have an angry outburst without body tension.

When you power map, your I-System is on, but your natural self, in executive mode, remains in charge as you keep mapping without directing your anger outward. Let your I-System run free as you jot down your thoughts, emotions, and body tension. As time goes on, you will see that your I-System will, over time, run out of steam as you keep mapping. You are finding your hidden requirements while exhausting your I-System. This shows you that you can deal with those impulses and mental pressures, and your body tension, without having harmful outbursts.

How did it go?

_____

_____

_____

_____

We all have an I-System, and we will never be rid of it. It's there to remind you of when you are off course (figure 2.1). It's your friend and your compass, telling you that you are not functioning in executive mode. Power mapping shows you that no matter how intense your I-System is, you can always be the boss of your I-System without acting in a destructive way.

CRISIS MANAGEMENT

1. Whenever and wherever you face a crisis, it's helpful to do a Crisis map. For this exercise, choose a crisis, big or small, in your life. Write the crisis in the oval. Take a couple of minutes to write around the oval whatever pops into your mind about how you can *handle* the crisis. Work quickly, without editing your thoughts. Your mind produces hundreds of thoughts each minute; the more open you are, the more insight you gain.

    ```
    ┌─────────────────────────────────────────────────────────┐
    │                      CRISIS MAP                           │
    └─────────────────────────────────────────────────────────┘
    ```

    MY CRISIS IS …

    _____

A. Is your mind cluttered or clear?

    _____

B. Describe your body tension:

    _____

C. What are your requirements?

    _____

    _____

D. How would you act in this mind-body state?

    _____

183

2. Do this map using your bridging awareness practices. Write the same crisis in the oval. Before you start writing about how you can *handle* the crisis, listen to any background sounds, feel your body's pressure on your seat, sense your feet on the floor, and feel the pen in your hand. Take your time. Once you feel settled, keep feeling the pen in your hand and start writing. Watch the ink go onto the paper, and listen to any background sounds. For the next few minutes, write down whatever thoughts pop into your mind about your crisis.

CRISIS MAP WITH BRIDGING

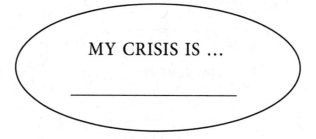

MY CRISIS IS ...

_____

A. What do you notice that is different on this map?

_____

B. How do you act with a quiet I-System?

_____

C. How will you defuse your requirements on the previous map when the situation arises again?

_____

_____

After doing the bridging map, if you still have body tension that relates to this situation, use power mapping. Remember, power mapping is only for people who have had success with using mind-body bridging practices in their daily lives.

WORST POSSIBLE THING

1. Take a few moments to consider the worst possible thing that can happen to you and write it in the oval. Now do a Worst Possible Thing That Can Happen to Me map. Write your thoughts around the oval for a couple of minutes. Describe your body tension at the bottom of the map.

WORST POSSIBLE THING THAT CAN HAPPEN TO ME MAP

THE WORST POSSIBLE
THING THAT CAN HAPPEN
TO ME IS

_____

Body Tension: _____

A. Looking at your map, list any signs of your active I-System:

_____

_____

B. List the requirements you find:

_____

_____

_____

2. Do this map again, writing the same thing in the oval. Before you start writing, use your bridging awareness practices. Listen to background sounds and feel your body's pressure on your seat, your feet on the floor, and the pen in your hand. Take your time. Once you are settled, keep feeling the pen in your hand as you start writing. Watch the ink go onto the paper and listen to background sounds. For the next few minutes, jot down any thoughts that come to mind about the worst possible thing that can happen to you.

**WORST POSSIBLE THING THAT CAN HAPPEN
TO ME MAP WITH BRIDGING**

THE WORST POSSIBLE
THING THAT CAN HAPPEN
TO ME IS
_____

A. What do you notice that's different on this map?

_____

_____

B. How do you act with a calm I-System?

_____

C. Defuse the requirements on your previous map. How did it go?

_____

_____

Your natural self is always with you, no matter what. Requirements are the only thing that stop you from experiencing and expressing your natural self.

PREVENTING ANGRY BEHAVIOR

1. Make a habit of using your mind-body bridging practices in your daily life (24/7), and do at least one map a day.

2. Use your body as a compass by noticing your personal and unique signs of body tension (tense jaw, clenched fist) that always come before your anger builds up. Then use all of your anger reduction tools and move into executive mode.

3. Use power mapping when you have stubbornly hidden requirements heating up your anger.

4. Live a full life with an I-System at rest.

PUTTING IT ALL TOGETHER

Luci, who was physically abused as a child, grew up with burning anger and would pick on and bully weaker playmates. Being quite bright, she did well in school, but her relationships with friends were shaky and filled with verbal explosions. She entered the army after college and was having a great career until she began to express her anger with her subordinates. After learning about mind-body bridging, she said, "My past started to become the past." She recognized that bullying was her fixer reacting to her depressor thoughts *I'm no good* and *I feel little*. She also began to realize that when anything happened that led her to believe that she was not in total control of a situation, it was her requirements for herself (*Be strong* and *Be in control*) that caused her distress. When she defused her requirements for others (*They should respect me*) her emotional outbursts stopped. She clearly saw that she was a victim of her I-System and its demands, rather than the behaviors of others or what was happening. Using all of her anger reduction tools, especially power mapping, her life changed. Her burning anger gave way to an inner strength and confidence, and her angry outbursts became a thing of the past.

You have now learned how to use all of your mind-body bridging anger reduction tools, and have mapped, recognized, and defused many of your requirements. These tools quiet your I-System so that you can manage any situation that comes up in your life without having angry outbursts. Remember, each moment that your I-System is in control of your anger is a moment filled with tension and powerlessness. When your natural self, in executive mode, is handling a situation, the choices you make guide you to your best life.

Anger Reduction Tools

➤ Use power mapping to map your way out of anger.

➤ Live life with an I-System that's at rest.

MBB RATING SCALE
MANAGE ANGER ANYTIME, ANYPLACE

Date: _____

After using the tools in this chapter for a few days, check the box that best describes your practice: hardly ever, sometimes, usually, almost always.

How often do you...	Hardly Ever	Sometimes	Usually	Almost Always
Listen to background sounds?				
Sense the sensation under your fingers when you take a drink?				
Experience gravity?				
Use bridging practices to bust stress or melt misery?				
Become really aware of your daily activities, like making the bed, eating, and driving?				
Hear the water going down the drain and experience the water on your body when you are showering or washing your hands?				
Use bridging to help you sleep?				
Use bridging to help you relax and stay focused?				
Notice body sensations as a sign of an active I-System?				
Realize that an active I-System is underlying your problem?				
Notice your depressor?				
Notice your fixer?				
Defuse your depressor?				
Defuse your fixer?				
Notice storylines?				
Realize that requirements are causing your daily upsets?				
Recognize and defuse your requirements?				
Notice when the powerless self is in charge?				
Realize that the powerless self is a myth of the I-System?				
Know when your natural self is in executive mode?				
Notice when your natural self is functioning moment by moment?				
Make daily mind-body maps?				
Use power mapping?				
Use your anger reduction tools?				
Live life in executive mode, with your natural self in charge?				

MBB QUALITY OF LIFE GAUGE

Date: _____

Only do this gauge when you have made a habit of using the anger reduction tools from this workbook in your life. Please compare your scores with those from the quality of life gauges in chapters 1 and 4. This gauge lets you measure your progress and keep track of your life-changing experiences.

Over the past seven days, how did you do in these areas?

Circle the number under your answer.	Not at all	Several days	More than half the days	Nearly every day
1. I've had positive interest and pleasure in my activities.	0	1	3	5
2. I've felt optimistic, excited, and hopeful.	0	1	3	5
3. I've slept well and woken up feeling refreshed.	0	1	3	5
4. I've had lots of energy.	0	1	3	5
5. I've been able to focus on tasks and use self-discipline.	0	1	3	5
6. I've stayed healthy, eaten well, exercised, and had fun.	0	1	3	5
7. I've felt good about my relationships with my family and friends.	0	1	3	5
8. I've been satisfied with my accomplishments at home, work, or school.	0	1	3	5
9. I've been comfortable with my financial situation.	0	1	3	5
10. I've felt good about the spiritual base of my life.	0	1	3	5
11. I've been satisfied with the direction of my life.	0	1	3	5
12. I've felt fulfilled, with a sense of well-being and peace of mind.	0	1	3	5

Score Key: Column Total   ____   ____   ____   ____

0-15 . . . . Poor

16-30 . . . . Fair   Total Score _____

31-45 . . . . .Good

46 and above . . . . Excellent

CONCLUSION

The design of this book is based on over a decade of research and clinical experience. Each mind-body bridging map you do adds to your ability to gain control of your anger. The appendixes of this book contain a two-part mapping template that you can use for your daily ongoing mapping practice. Mapping gives you insight into what is happening in your life right here, right now. When you use your anger reduction tools (listed below), your inner power, wisdom, and beauty flow into your everyday life.

Anger Reduction Tools

CHAPTER 1

➤ *Recognize when your I-System is active or inactive.*

➤ *Use thought labeling.*

➤ *Use bridging awareness practices:*

- *Awareness of background sounds*

- *Awareness of what you are touching*

- *Awareness of colors, facial features, shapes*

- *Awareness of your body sensations*

CHAPTER 2

➤ *Create two-part mind-body maps.*

➤ *Discover requirements that activate your I-System.*

➤ *Recognize requirements to quiet your I-System.*

➤ *Use your body as a compass by befriending your body.*

CHAPTER 3

➤ *Uncover your negative thoughts and feelings about yourself.*

➤ *Recognize the depressor's activity.*

➤ *Become aware of your storylines.*

➤ *Defuse the depressor.*

CHAPTER 4

> ➤ *Defuse the fixer.*

> ➤ *Recognize the depressor/fixer cycle.*

> ➤ *Convert fixer activity to executive functioning.*

CHAPTER 5

> ➤ *Defuse your requirements for others and for situations.*

CHAPTER 6

> ➤ *Defuse your requirements for yourself.*

> ➤ *Defuse your requirements for your relationships.*

CHAPTER 7

> ➤ *Defuse requirements to allow proper self-care and support wellness.*

> ➤ *Uncover and use your MBB action steps for self-care and wellness.*

CHAPTER 8

> ➤ *Use the Five MBB Steps for Conflict Reduction.*

> ➤ *Uncover and use MBB action steps to reduce conflicts.*

CHAPTER 9

> ➤ *Use power mapping to map your way out of anger.*

> ➤ *Live life with an I-System at rest.*

Congratulations on completing this workbook! You have gained a unique freedom: the ability to live your life in executive mode with an I-System at rest. With the anger reduction tools you have learned in this workbook, you can now live your best life with your natural self in charge.

Appendix A:
Mind-Body Bridging
Daily Mapping Guide

1. Choose a mapping topic and write it in the oval. It may be as simple as "What's on my mind?" or as specific as a certain troubling situation. Next, take a couple of minutes to write around the oval your thoughts about that topic. Be specific. Describe your body tension at the bottom of the map.

CHOOSE YOUR TOPIC MAP

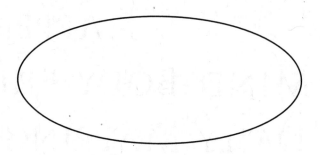

Body Tension: _____

Look at what your overactive I-System is doing.

A. What are your depressors?

_____

B. What are your fixers?

_____

C. What are your storylines?

_____

D. What are your requirements?

_____

E. How do you act in this mind-body state?

_____

2. Do this map again using bridging awareness practices. Write the same topic in the oval. Before you start writing about the topic, listen to background sounds and feel your body's pressure on your seat, your feet on the floor, and the pen in your hand. Take your time. Once you are settled, keep feeling the pen in your hand as you start writing. Watch the ink go onto the paper, and keep listening to background sounds. Write for a couple of minutes.

CHOOSE YOUR TOPIC MAP WITH BRIDGING

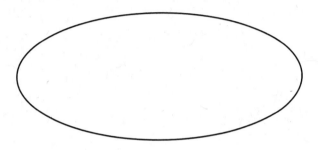

A. How is this map the same as or different from the previous one?

_____

_____

B. How do you act in this mind-body state?

_____

_____

C. Are you able to defuse the requirements on the previous map?

_____

_____

Remember, it's either your powerless self or your natural self in the driver's seat. You choose.

Appendix B: Mind-Body Language

CHAPTER 1

I-System: Each of us has an I-System, and it's either active (on) or resting (off). You know the I-System is active when your mind is cluttered with spinning thoughts, your body is tense, and you are getting irritated and angry. It's called the "I-System," because it prompts you to falsely identify with the spinning thoughts and the physical distress the I-System causes.

Natural self: How you think, feel, see the world, and act when your I-System is resting and you are functioning in executive mode. Your mind and body work in harmony as a unit, and stressors are handled smoothly and quickly, without angry outbursts.

Mind-body bridging: When you use the tools in this workbook, you form a bridge from your active I-System (where angry outbursts happen) to your natural self in executive mode (where daily life is handled in a smooth and healthy way).

CHAPTER 2

Requirements: Thoughts made into mental rules by your I-System that tell you how you and the world should be in each moment. When your I-System rules are broken, you become upset and angry.

Recognize requirements: When you become clearly aware that *your requirement,* not the events around you, is making your I-System active, you reduce your anger and function in executive mode.

CHAPTER 3

Powerless self: How you think, feel, see the world, and act when your I-System is active. Life is overwhelming, your executive functioning is impaired, and you struggle vainly to manage your anger.

Depressor: A part of the I-System that takes your natural negative thoughts and self-talk (things you say to yourself), and creates body tension and mind clutter. It makes you feel weak, powerless, and ready to explode.

Storyline: Thoughts that your I-System spins into stories (true or not) that keep your I-System going; they pull you away from the here and now. This can make your anger build up and cause you to make bad decisions.

Defusing the depressor: When you become clearly aware that your negative thoughts are "just thoughts," those thoughts then do not create body tension and mind clutter.

CHAPTER 4

Fixer: The depressor's partner that pushes you with overactive, never-ending thoughts of how to fix yourself and the world. All your angry and destructive outbursts are fixer driven.

Defusing the fixer: When you become clearly aware (at the time you are doing something) that your fixer is active and use your anger reduction tools, you take away the fixer's power. Right away, you feel a shift from a stressful, angry state to one with a ready and relaxed mind and body. You can now calmly take care of yourself and whatever you have to do in executive mode.

Depressor/fixer cycle: These I-System partners create a vicious cycle, keep the I-System going and going, and cause your angry and harmful actions.

CHAPTER 5

Defusing requirements: When you use all your anger reduction tools, you handle a situation that used to make your I-System active with a ready and relaxed mind and body. Even when the picture of how you and the world should be is not fulfilled, the requirement is powerless to turn on your I-System.

CHAPTER 7

Mind-body bridging (MBB) action steps: Actions you take to achieve a goal that come from the two-part mind-body mapping process, and are carried out by your natural self in executive mode.

REFERENCES

Beck, J. S. 1995. *Cognitive Therapy: Basics and Beyond.* 1st ed. New York: The Guilford Press.

Block, S. H., and C. B. Block. 2007. *Come to Your Senses: Demystifying the Mind-Body Connection.* 2nd ed. New York: Atria Books/Beyond Words Publishing.

Block, S. H., and C. B. Block. 2010. *Mind-Body Workbook for PTSD: A 10-Week Program for Healing After Trauma.* Oakland, CA: New Harbinger Publications.

Block, S. H., and C. B. Block. 2012. *Mind-Body Workbook for Stress: Effective Tools for Lifelong Stress Reduction and Crisis Management.* With A. A. Peters. Oakland, CA: New Harbinger Publications.

Block, S. H., S. H. Ho, and Y. Nakamura. 2009. "A Brain Basis for Transforming Consciousness with Mind-Body Bridging." Abstract 93. Paper presented at Toward a Science of Consciousness Conference, June 12, at Hong Kong Polytechnical University, Hong Kong.

Boly, M., C. Phillips, E. Balteau, C. Schnakers, C. Degueldre, G. Moonen, A. Luxen, P. Peigneux, M. E. Faymonville, P. Maquet, and S. Laureys. 2008. "Consciousness and Cerebral Baseline Activity Fluctuations." *Human Brain Mapping* 29(7): 868–74.

Boly, M., C. Phillips, L. Tshibanda, A. Vanhaudenhuyse, M. Schabus, T. T. Dang-Vu, G. Moonen, R. Hustinx, P. Maquet, and S. Laureys. 2008. "Intrinsic Brain Activity in Altered States of Consciousness: How Conscious Is the Default Mode of Brain Function?" *Annals of the New York Academy of Sciences* 1129: 119–29.

Dutton, D. G., and D. J. Sonkin. 2002. *Intimate Violence: Contemporary Treatment Innovations.* Binghamton, NY: The Haworth Maltreatment and Trauma Press.

Lee, M. Y., A. Uken, and J. Sebold. 2004. "Accountability for Change: Solution-Focused Treatment with Domestic Violence Offenders." *Families in Society* 85(4): 463–76.

Linehan, M. M. 1993. *Cognitive-Behavioral Treatment of Borderline Personality Disorder.* New York: The Guilford Press.

Lipschitz, D. L., R. Kuhn, A. Y. Kinney, G. W. Donaldson, and Y. Nakamura. 2013. "Reduction in Salivary Alpha-Amylase Levels Following Mind-Body Interventions in Cancer Survivors: An Exploratory Study." *Psychoneuroendocrinology.*

Nakamura, Y., D. L. Lipschitz, R. Kuhn, A. Y. Kinney, and G. W. Donaldson. 2013. "Investigating Efficacy of Two Brief Mind-Body Intervention Programs for Managing Sleep Disturbance in Cancer Survivors: A Pilot Randomized Controlled Trial." *Journal of Cancer Survivorship*, 7(2):165–82.

Nakamura, Y., D. L. Lipschitz, R. Landward, R. Kuhn, and G. West. 2011. "Two Sessions of Sleep-Focused Mind-Body Bridging Improve Self-Reported Symptoms of Sleep and PTSD in Veterans: A Pilot Randomized Controlled Trial." *Journal of Psychosomatic Research* 70(4): 335–45.

Rosenberg, M. S. 2003. "Voices from the Group: Domestic Violence Offenders' Experience of Intervention." *Journal of Aggression, Maltreatment, and Trauma* 7(1–2): 305–17.

Tollefson, D. R., K. Webb, D. Shumway, S. H. Block, and Y. Nakamura. 2009. "A Mind-Body Approach to Domestic Violence Perpetrator Treatment: Program Overview and Preliminary Outcomes." *Journal of Aggression, Maltreatment, and Trauma* 18(1):17–45.

Weissman, D. H., K. C. Roberts, K. M. Visscher, and M. G. Woldorff. 2006. "The Neural Bases of Momentary Lapses in Attention." *Nature Neuroscience* 9(7): 971–78.

Williams, M., J. Teasdale, Z. Segal, and J. Kabat-Zinn. 2007. *The Mindful Way Through Depression: Freeing Yourself from Chronic Unhappiness.* New York: The Guilford Press.

Stanley H. Block, MD, is adjunct professor of psychiatry at the University of Utah School of Medicine, and a board-certified psychiatrist and psychoanalyst. He is a consultant on the medical staff at US Army and Veterans Administration Hospitals. He lectures and consults with treatment centers worldwide and is coauthor of *Mind-Body Workbook for Stress, Mind-Body Workbook for PTSD,* and *Come to Your Senses.* He and his wife, Carolyn Bryant Block, live in Copalis Beach, WA. Find out more about his work online at mindbodybridging.com.

Carolyn Bryant Block is coauthor of *Bridging the I-System, Come to Your Senses, Mind-Body Workbook for PTSD,* and *Mind-Body Workbook for Stress.* She is also the co-developer of mind-body bridging and identity system (I-System) theory and techniques.

Andrea A. Peters is an educator certified in mind-body bridging. She guided the organizational development of mind-body bridging material.

Foreword writer **Derrik R. Tollefson, PhD**, is associate professor and coordinator of the MSW program at Utah State University. He teaches courses on family violence and frequently provides training on this topic.